The Unfathomable Hand of Destiny

Or, is it Free Will?

Bhupendra Suri

INDIA • SINGAPORE • MALAYSIA

To my late father Lt. Col. Gurdial Singh Suri,
who provided me with profound love, unwavering
support, and also the freedom and wings to fly.

Contents

Part III
Krishna

Acknowledgments

I want to express my deepest gratitude to the people who have made this journey possible and whose love and support have been my guiding lights.

I dedicate this book to my incredible father, Gurdial Singh Suri, whom I lost a couple of months back. Dad, you were a rock-solid support during all the difficult phases of my life. Your wisdom and guidance have shaped me into who I am today, and I am forever thankful to you. You will be dearly missed. Your love and influence will remain in my heart always.

I must also thank my mother, Kuljit Suri, who always took out the time to read the draft copies of my books. Her insightful feedback and suggestions helped me refine my work and ensure my message came across as effectively as possible. Your perspective and guidance are always invaluable, Mom, and I am deeply grateful for your constant support.

To my loving wife, Harpreet, thank you for your unwavering support, patience, and belief in me. You have sacrificed so much, especially the quality time you would have otherwise had with me, while I was busy with my projects. Thank you for always being there for me, like a solid, dependable rock, and for your patience, love, and understanding.

My two amazing sons, Rohtash and Sukhman, gave up a lot of their time—time that should have been theirs—to support me in completing these projects. They did this not only with acceptance but with cheerful encouragement, often helping me along the way. Thank you, Rohtash and Sukhman, for your unwavering support and for being such an integral part of this journey.

To my brother, Jasjeet Suri, thank you for all those long-drawn discussions and debates we've had. Your insights and perspectives have helped me think through the complex question of the existence of free will. Your presence in my life is a constant source of strength, and I am grateful for our conversations that always challenge me to think deeper.

A special shout-out to my niece, Jasnee, who helped me with the cover design and contributed the brilliant idea of depicting the hand of destiny on the cover. Your creativity and vision were instrumental in bringing this book to life in a visually powerful way. Thank you for your invaluable input!

This book reflects the love, encouragement, and inspiration I receive from all of you. I am truly blessed to have such a remarkable family by my side.

Introduction

I wrote this book many years ago, but it remained in hibernation for a long time. Being an engineer and business management student, I am usually hard-wired to complete what I start and am pretty task-oriented. However, this book remained in inertia for a very long time, almost three years. I did not know why, but slowly, the truth dawned on me as I started working on two projects in the interim, where my thinking evolved. Some critical pieces of the jigsaw puzzle were missing in my earlier manuscript, but my work on my last two books, *Every Grain has a Name* and *I to Infinity*, helped me unlock them. Today, as I complete this manuscript, I realise that this slowdown in this project was part of the larger game plan of the universe. I will explain how.

The big question I have struggled with over two decades is whether free will exists. Simple as this question may sound, the answer is incredibly complex. So please bear with me for a few moments while I explain. This question popped stubbornly into my mind almost 20 years ago after a bizarre dream. It was an early morning dream. I dreamt that I was slowly and languidly moving up and down. Each movement was so slow that it seemed like an eternity. I felt I was creating this movement through my thoughts and actions. I was sometimes feeling happy and occasionally concerned at this constant languid movement. This entire process went on for a long time (though time is a relative thing in a dream). After some time, I saw a more expansive vision come to life. I noticed I was a mere fly on the side of the cart wheel trundling along the village road. I remember feeling quite surprised that I was in no way responsible for all my experiences.

The cart was moving with its purpose, and I was just experiencing the movement despite myself. For some strange reason, I did not find it odd that I was a fly, and the experience and feelings I was going through were quite human. In that dream, everything seemed perfectly fine and logical. The dream was extremely vivid and real. I have not felt so deeply engaged in every little nuance of an experience, even during waking hours. I got up with a start, remembering every detail in the dream, and tried to make some sense. What did it mean?

The answer dawned soon as I meditated on it for some time. Was my life like a fly on the cart wheel, where I thought things were happening because I was deciding and doing certain things using my 'free will,' but in reality, a much larger movement was going on with a far more profound purpose? A purpose that I would never understand until I could get a much more comprehensive worldview. This thought stuck with me for many years. I started to write a daily morning diary and reflect on such philosophical ideas. If this worldview was accurate, then my experience of free will was an illusion. Things were happening as expected, and I was mistakenly assuming responsibility for things I was not responsible for, just like the fly on the cart wheel.

As an engineer, I researched what the scientists were saying about free will. At that time, I was surprised to find a similar view dominant in the world of science that *there is no free will but only an illusion of free will that we experience.* For example, the scientists quoted experiments where, by attaching electrodes to a subject's head, they could predict—many moments before even the individual is conscious of it—when they would make a voluntary move, like moving a finger. This means that forces within the system make decisions, and the individual ego takes post facto ownership of the same. This view asserted that all the physical and mental forces move us from moment to moment, choicelessly like robots. This current thinking points to a deterministic universe. There are many counterviews to such experiments in the world of science, but my goal is not to take you to the depth of this 'free will' discussion in the introduction itself. Instead, it is simply to share some perspectives that exist out there on this issue of free will.

Personally, I could not easily buy this argument of a fully deterministic universe where everything was predetermined and destined. It was as if the creator had switched on the start button, and then things would follow through choicelessly, with an illusion of free will, which we all experience and cannot deny. So, for me, the search continued. This search took me down the alleyway of quantum mechanics, many dimensions of Western and Eastern philosophy, and some fascinating insights arrived. I shared these in my first book, A Fly on the Cart Wheel. However, the problem of the existence or non-existence of individual free will was not conclusively resolved; instead, another dimension of a Universal Will driving everything entered the equation.

This possibility brought the question that if no individual free will existed, but only a Universal Will, then we are just puppets like Mario in the video game, driven by the player's will outside the game. Further, if the future is fixed or predestined, what is the purpose of any Universal free will that plays out a fixed movie choicelessly? Free will implies the execution of choice between alternatives, but if the movie or game script is written in advance and is not allowed to change, where is the choice? Even if a Universal will has written the script, now it is forced to execute it choicelessly. On the other hand, if individual free will exists, what is the relationship between the individual and the Universal will, and how do they interact?

Many years ago, I undertook the current project where I attempted to look at this issue from the eyes of the characters of Duryodhana, Yudhishthira, and Krishna. The idea was to look at these ideas from the lives of some well-known personalities in the Mahabharatha and make these theoretical discussions on free will somewhat human. This manuscript hibernated for three years. Initially, I was unsure what prevented me from taking this book project forward, but later, I realised that some critical aspects were not closed in my thinking on the nature of reality and the existence/non-existence of free will. Deep insights and multiple leaps in my thinking occurred in the intervening years, which were summarised in my two previous books. These insights were essential as I reopened the old project (the current book) and brought it to closure.

Interestingly, while there was one large last leap that I did close in the above two books on how the Universal will and individual will co-exist, I still felt that the step was closed somewhat theoretically. In the current book, the maximum changes in the recent months leading to the closure of this project happened in the last part of this book as I tried to see this world from the eyes of Krishna. I feel this book humanises the learnings of my previous books and makes them real. This book will open your mind to the possibility that you may have manifested the entire range of experiences that constitute your life and the fact that everything is flexible in your life: your past, present, and future! However, this does not mean that the "fly on the cart wheel view" of the world is wrong or inaccurate. These are just stages in the development of human consciousness that all beings would go through within a single or multiple lifetimes. These are also stages of a natural evolution until full realisation and a steady state of flow arrive.

In my older days, as I mentioned before, I would have pushed for specific outcomes at specific times and fretted about delays, but not so anymore. My personal evolution as I concluded these books and the flow of certain events have confirmed that sometimes we need to let things be and listen to the soft footsteps of the universe. Be calm and patient, and let the answers come on their own. Most importantly, these answers **always** come, but only at the right time when we are ripe enough to absorb them. My most significant learning was that forces much larger than us drive things in the universe. Still, it is essential to note that we are not puppets and have a serious role to play in this evolutionary process.

As you go through the characters of Duryodhana, Yudhisthira, and Krishna, you will see this evolution from the individual will to the Universal will and then back to the individual, but on a very different scale. I believe this is the journey of the evolution of every individual. We all have to go through it and are active participants in the process. I hope this book can help you in your journey, wherever you may be along this path today.

Best wishes as you travel through time with these timeless characters. May the Force be with you!

Part I

Duryodhana

"There's nowhere you can be that isn't where you're meant to be..."

— John Lennon

Chapter One

The Game of Dice

The atmosphere in the court was highly charged and tense. His breathing was shallow as he looked at the person shaking his hand to roll the dice. He knew his time had come. He had longed for this moment for a very long time. He remembered all the humiliation he had faced at the hands of his opponents. These people had taken away what rightfully belonged to him. The kingdom had always been his. These people wrongfully claimed it. He specifically disliked his sister-in-law, who had always looked down upon him. He could imagine her laughing behind his back, joking with her friends and maids about her uncouth brother-in-law. Now, it was his turn, and they would remember this humiliation for the rest of their lives. He felt exultant!

The dice rolled onto the floor, all eyes looking on expectantly to see the number that appeared on the top face. His opponents, of course, watched anxiously. Their whole lives depended on the roll of these dice. They had already gone too far and lost most of what belonged to them—their wealth, their kingdom—and now they seemed to be on the verge of losing everything.

Overnight, they would go from being kings to slaves. The situation was like a terrible dream they could not awaken from. Everything in the world seemed to have turned against them.

Duryodhana looked at his perspiring opponents, enjoying their discomfort. He knew the game was rigged and that his victory was inevitable. He had spent his entire life imagining ways to humiliate them, though so far, unsuccessfully. His opponents always seemed to escape the most difficult situations through some twist of fate, but not this time. This time, he would have his revenge, not behind anybody's back nor through any intrigue that they could turn around at the last minute. This victory would occur publicly and gloriously in front of the entire world. This final revenge on them would break their backs once and for all.

Duryodhana had never felt equally or fairly treated in the presence of the Pandavas. He could see it in the eyes of his gurus and even the normally nonpartisan Bhishma Pitahmah. Their eyes would subtly soften when the Pandavas came into their presence but hardened when he tried to say something. Why this difference? He had never been able to understand. Was he not one of the direct descendants of the Kurus? Was he not a brave warrior who had also put in much effort to master the art of the mace—was he not the best at it? Was he not the first son of the eldest son of the previous King? So what if his father was blind and had been politically sidelined by Vidur and forced to give up his throne in favour of his younger brother? That sly fox, Vidur, was very dangerous. He claimed to know right or wrong in every situation, which he argued by eloquently quoting the scriptures, traditions, and the various rules of the land.

Duryodhana had seen that Vidur could get the larger court to agree on almost anything by generating all kinds of abstruse logic and arguments. Nobody had the guts to challenge him with the considerable credibility he had built over the years. He always demonstrated feigned humility, showing that he was only committed to truth and righteousness and always concerned about the future safety and welfare of the Hastinapur state. Even today, if anybody could disrupt his plan, it was Vidur.

The more he thought of Vidur and all that had been wrongfully taken from him, the more he burned internally. He was abruptly transported into the past when he and his clan, the Kauravas, were abruptly thrown out of power by a few deft strokes of political intrigue. But long before that, there was the even more painful reality of his birth. It was as though everything in the universe seemed to conspire against him at every step, trying to stop him from getting his due.

Chapter Two

An Unnatural Birth

His had not been a natural birth. He and his 99 brothers had been in their mother's womb simultaneously, thanks to a blessing given by the great sage Ved Vyasa. During her younger years, his mother took great care of the sage when he visited their kingdom. Extremely pleased with her service and devotion, he had blessed her thus. Much later in her life, his mother had taken a vow to blindfold herself as an act of sacrifice and deference to her blind husband, King Dhritarashtra—a decision he could never understand. Having a blind father was bad enough, but a blind mother further compounded the situation!

They were in their mother's womb for over 16 months—at least, that is what he had heard from the palace gossip. Nobody could understand what was going on. After 16 months of waiting, even their mother lost patience with the way things were going and asked her maid to hit her belly with a stick to get the baby out. Of course, no one knew what was really going on at that time. The maid was horrified at the task set by the Queen and had to be bullied into complying. A couple of solid strikes later, a big blob of flesh came out of his mother's belly. The maid was amazed, as it looked nothing like a human foetus. A hushed silence fell over the room as the maid did not have the guts to tell her Queen what had come out of her belly.

"Why are you so quiet? Tell me what happened," demanded the Queen. The maid did her best to explain to the blindfolded Queen what the issue was, and slowly, the enormity of the situation dawned on the ladies.

His blind father, Dhritarashtra, was summoned, and when he felt the ball of flesh, he was shocked. Doctors were called in, and they were equally confused. Finally, Sage Vyas was called to guide the family through this horrible crisis. The sage looked at the giant ball of flesh, smiled, and said, "Don't worry, your children will be fine." Gandhari and Dhritarashtra heard this statement and could not believe their ears. How could such a learned sage call this blob of flesh children? Both of them were blind, but their sense of touch and feel had given them a good sense of how bad the situation was.

Dhritarashtra asked the sage to explain what he meant. The sage smiled and said, "Dear King, you should understand that my blessings never go to waste." Then, Gandhari recounted the entire episode of when Vyasa had blessed her with a hundred sons. "Don't worry," said the sage gently. "These are just a hundred foetuses born a bit too early. All you need to do now is put them into separate clay pots with ghee and keep the room's temperature as high as it would be in a woman's body. Soon, they will be born fine. The day they break out of the clay pots will be the time and day of their actual birth."

Everyone in the room listened incredulously. The sage had never been wrong in the past, and they were sure what he was saying would be true, irrespective of how bizarre it sounded. Suddenly, Dhritarashtra got very animated, issuing urgent instructions to all present. He was very concerned about his hundred sons lest anything untoward happened to them. Everybody was running around, getting the fires started to heat the room. As guided by the sage, clay pots were prepared, and soon, everything was as the sage had asked. Gandhari had always wanted a daughter and asked the sage if this was possible. The sage obliged, and one extra piece was cut, making it one hundred and one pieces. The last piece would be the only sister of the Kauravas, Dushala.

Gandhari was relieved by what the sage had said but was still worried about her children's future. Would they survive this crazy birth? She had never heard or seen anything like this before. She had waited long to be able to hold her child to her bosom after its birth. But this was an altogether different experience, and she was quite apprehensive. She could not voice her worries in public as that would be seen as highly disrespectful to the great sage, but she continuously did so to her husband.

Dhritarashtra tried his best to comfort her while he himself worried about how all this would end.

Blindness had made both of them highly dependent on information coming from others, which they could not verify themselves. This time, they felt even more helpless as people worked around them and kept reassuring them that everything was under control. They could not make sure firsthand that things were really in order. But then, this was their due.

Dhritarashtra had always felt that Gandhari had made the wrong choice in choosing to blindfold herself. He had hoped that she would be his eyes and he would have seen the world through her. But now, they were both blind and dependent on others. Gandhari felt that if she could see when her husband could not, her status would be perceived to be higher than her husband's, and that was not right. She thought she would never be able to appreciate and experience his frustrations if she did not blindfold herself. This was the only way they would be genuinely bonded as one. Anyway, there was no going back once she had taken the vow. These were just hypothetical thoughts; this is how it was to be, and they waited expectantly for their sons' births.

Many months passed with no changes to the pots. The temperature in the room was maintained at quite a high level, as one would expect inside a human body. The Queen prayed fervently for the successful births of her sons. Finally, one day, when the Queen and the King were sitting together, the maid rushed in to inform them that there was movement in one of the clay pots and that it was showing cracks. Both of them immediately rushed to the room. They could hear the sounds of one of the clay pots cracking open. Many key people from the court had also joined them. Everyone had been waiting for the King's sons to be born. The pundits were there to record the date and time of the births.

And then it happened. Quite suddenly, the fire in the room flared up dangerously. The blind King and Queen felt the sudden surge of heat intensity. There were screams from some of the maids—it seemed the fire had gone out of control. The King was very disturbed; how could somebody be so careless, especially at such a crucial moment? He shouted in anger at the guards, "Put the fire out immediately. Who is responsible for being so careless at such a time? I will have their head!" People ran around, redoubling their efforts, and the fire was brought under control.

But then reports from all parts of the city started to pour in. Courtiers rushed in to tell the King that fires were breaking out all over the kingdom and that these bursts of flame were intense and difficult to control. Then came more news of jackals howling during the day and an earthquake in the city. These were not good omens. While the King ordered immediate action to stop the fires, he focused on the impending birth of his first son. And soon enough, the clay pot broke, and a small child slithered out of it. He was handed over to his mother, Gandhari. She felt a deep surge of love as she moved her hand over the child and felt his features. She longed to have a look at him, but the vow she had taken prevented that; this was indeed her most challenging moment. The King also reached out and touched the child, and there were tears in his eyes.

At that moment, the kul-guru[1], Kripacharya, spoke up, "O King! I have just read the horoscope of this child. I am afraid I don't have good news."

The King, startled, asked, "What news?"

Kripacharya continued, "Dear King, I know you love your son beyond measure, but the horoscope clearly says that he brings nothing but doom for the Kuru clan."

The King was dumbfounded; he could not believe what he had heard. Gandhari's heart sank; could her firstborn indeed bring the destruction of her entire clan? She could not understand why. "Are you sure?" asked the King. "This is a very bold assertion to make!"

"Yes, my King. My job is to let you know the truth. I have checked and rechecked all the calculations. There is no doubt in what I just said."

There was silence in the room. And that is when Vidur spoke, "Dear brother, the omens are very bad, and

---

1   Kulguru – family priest

so in the best interest of Hastinapur and the Kuru clan, I think the child should not be allowed to live. You will have other children from the other clay pots and still have many sons. I know it sounds extremely wrong at the moment, but it is best for our future."

Duryodhana had heard of this story and knew that Vidur had wanted him dead even at that time. Only his father's decision saved him, and he had managed to live to see this day. He could not believe that his father's wisest counsel had asked him to get rid of his firstborn, the child he had waited for so long.

Shakuni, his mother's brother and his closest confidant—the only person that Duryodhana believed had his best interests at heart—always told him to be wary of Vidur, and rightly so. The man was ready to kill him when he was just a newborn child, following those all-too-vague premonitions. He must have something against him or his family. He repeatedly saw this pattern throughout his childhood in different forms and situations.

Chapter Three

Pandu's Curse and the Boons of Kunti

Duryodhana was confident Vidur was very biased towards Pandu and his sons, the Pandavas. He had seen the evidence of this behaviour in multiple instances. While Vidur claimed to be impartial in every situation, this was untrue. Duryodhana felt he was lucky to have his Uncle Shakuni by his side, who had shown him the bias in Vidur's decisions throughout his childhood. Even before Duryodhana was born, some events demonstrated this bias.

Dhritarashtra was the elder of the two sons of the Kuru king, Vichitravirya, but had been born blind. Vichitravirya died, and Dhritarashtra was next in line, but Vidur convinced Bhishma to declare Pandu as the next King, citing that Dhritarashtra was not fit to rule because of his blindness. Hence, Pandu was proclaimed King after Vichitravirya's death. Though Pandu had always been respectful towards his brother, the pain of not getting what was due to him always rankled Dhritarashtra, but he had reconciled to the situation.

Some years later, Pandu committed a serious offence of killing a sage by mistake when he was out on a hunt. He mistook him for a deer in the bushes. Being a very upright king, to repent for his deed, he left for the forest after abdicating his throne in favour of Dhritarashtra. That is how Dhritarashtra became a king, while Pandu, his first wife, Kunti, and his second wife, Madri, retired to the forest. The five Pandavas were born in the forest. When Pandu died, the Pandavas returned to Hastinapur to study under the tutelage of Drona. That was when the Kauravas and the Pandavas started to live and study together. Unfortunately, it was not the best of relationships.

Duryodhana knew the story of the birth of his cousins, which was very relevant, especially in decisions of kingship. What troubled Duryodhana most was how Vidur always selectively picked facts to favour ideas that he supported. Vidur knew well that the Pandavas were not Pandu's biological descendants. The curse Pandu had received from the sage he had mistakenly killed was that he would die if he got intimate with any woman, including his wife. Everyone knew of this curse on Pandu. Surprisingly, the Pandavas were born despite Pandu being under the curse. Duryodhana had heard some interesting stories on this count.

It was believed that Kunti had a boon from Sage Durvasa that she could invoke any God and bear children from them just by uttering a mantra. The story going around was that all the Pandavas had taken birth through this process, given the curse on their father. Duryodhana was sceptical about this story but did not question it more than required. But he could not understand why Vidur, who had found logic and arguments to have him killed as a child or keep his father away from the throne, was not questioning the legitimacy of Yudhisthira as the next King of Hastinapur, even though he was not a direct descendant of Pandu? Such hypocrisy! He knew if he confronted Vidur with this fact, Vidur would come up with some arcane technical response based on some historical scriptures and manage to justify his position. It was a waste of time.

The only person he could confide in was his uncle, Shakuni. Shakuni listened to Duryodhan's apprehensions and responded with a smile, "Dear nephew, I am glad you have also reached the same conclusion. People desire to do things and use convenient arguments to support their desires. And when it is people like Vidur, who have mastered the art of dialogue, it seems as if no one could be more unbiased and righteous than them, even when they're simply following their desires or biases. The funny part is that they genuinely believe that they are being objective and righteous. If you present counterarguments like these, they will simply come up with another set of arguments; it is an unending process and a complete waste of time. This is the only truth. Nothing is fundamentally right or wrong; it is all about what you desire. Be strong in your desire, and you will surely rule Hastinapur. Once you are firmly established as King, even Vidur's arguments will turn in your favour. This world belongs to the powerful. Those in power make the rules, and arguments are generated to support their actions. The key is getting the seat of power."

Duryodhana knew Shakuni was right. He was deeply concerned about his father. The equation could change overnight if the current band of biased courtiers misled his weak, indecisive father. The Pandavas would get the upper hand, and all power would rest in their hands. And the powerful would write history as they wished.

Chapter Four

Tense Growing Up Years

Duryodhana thanked his stars that he'd had his Uncle Shakuni by his side in his youth to help him understand all the political intricacies and keep him vigilant about the hostile forces around him. Shakuni was his mother's brother. It was customary that a close relative of the bride came with her to the groom's house till the new bride settled in. Shakuni had overstayed his visit and had become a full-time member of the Hastinapur royal family. Shakuni was determined that Duryodhana be the next King after Dhritarashtra, and he would not leave till he had achieved that purpose. Even Dhritarashtra wanted this to happen in his heart of hearts.

Duryodhana knew that Yudhishthira was older than him by one year and could come and claim the throne, and this rankled him to no end. Should not the ruling King's eldest son be the next King? Yes, there was the argument that the real King was Pandu, who had just given the reins to his blind elder brother, Dhritarashtra, to hold in his stead while he was in the forest on penance. Dhritarashtra was just a regent for his brother Pandu, not the real King.

According to Duryodhana, all this was just a play of words, just machinations of people like Vidur. Duryodhana knew he would go to any extent to achieve what he desired. Uncle Shakuni had always told him that there would be many forces out to destroy his future, and he had to make himself mentally tough and strong to withstand all of them. He had to be the King under any circumstances. He could not afford to get thrown off track by the myriad political court battles. King Dhritrashtra wanted this outcome in his heart, so who could stop that?

His weak spot was his mother, who was too soft and very inclusive, especially where the Pandavas were concerned. She had always told him that the kingship of Hastinapur would be decided based on the person's qualities and popularity among the people. So he should not take it for granted that he would be King. He always had this grouse with his mother about why she had covered her eyes even when she had normal eyes. Did she not care about her children? Yes, she had received many accolades from everyone for her brave step, but what about the young Kauravas being brought up by blind parents? Would she ever understand all the politics that was being played within the court to hold their family back in the race to the throne? He did not believe so.

He felt that she was living in her utopian world and just too nice to understand the brutal ways of the world. To compound the issue further, she had eliminated the possibility of getting the whole picture by tying the handkerchief around her eyes. He mostly ignored her. In a nutshell, Uncle Shakuni became the guiding light of his life and his source of real understanding of the world. They spent a lot of time together as Shakuni became both his father and mother.

Though physically, Shakuni was a short man with a twisted leg and walked with a limp; he was incredibly witty and intelligent. He had a natural grasp of human intentions, and he would immediately be able to understand the truth even when people played with words to hide their true intentions. Most importantly, he was the one person who thought only of Duryodhana's benefit. Duryodhana sincerely thanked God for this one boon in his life.

When the Pandavas returned from the forest with their mother after their father passed away, they were enrolled in Guru Kripacharya's Gurukul. Later, they were also tutored by Guru Dronacharya. Of the five Pandavas, Duryodhana hated Bhima the most. Bhima was an oversized bully who terrorised the Kaurava brothers all the time. Only he (Duryodhana) could stand up to Bhima and keep him in check, even though only somewhat.

Bhima fully reciprocated the animosity towards Duryodhana. They were both at loggerheads most of the time. There was never a single day when Bhima would not terrorise one of his 99 brothers. He would pull their hair until it hurt and sometimes even drag them around by their hair. If he managed to get one of his brothers alone, he would kick or thrash him for no reason, making fun of their weakness. He would do this when no elders were around, and as soon as it got reported to some elders, he would behave as if he were innocent and claim that the Kauravas were simply making up stories. He was insufferable, and Duryodhana vowed to teach him a lesson.

Then there was the eldest Pandava, Yudhishthira, whom Duryodhana felt was an apology for a man, who always compromised and agreed with everyone. He sucked up to the gurus and the elders endlessly, and as a result, he was loved by them. Duryodhana found it sickening. Leadership meant making tough decisions and changing the status quo, not being nice to everyone all the time, and doing all the right things as expected by society. There were rumours that both the gurus had recommended to the King that Yudhishthira would make a great king. Duryodhana could not believe it! Making a wimp like him the King of Hastinapur would be a great disaster.

Arjuna, the third brother, was the one person Duryodhana was most jealous of. Arjuna—a very focused and capable student—was the favourite of all the gurus. Dedicating umpteen hours to practice, he was turning out to be one of the most excellent archers of all time. While Duryodhana himself was a master of the mace and possibly one of the best at it, he knew Arjuna would be a formidable foe on the battlefield. Of all the Pandavas, only he (Arjuna) could hold off an entire army alone. So Duryodhana was jealous and also a little afraid of him.

But of all the brothers, his worst relationship was with Bhima. The feelings were mutual, and this hatred ran very deep, to the extent that Duryodhana even plotted to get Bhima killed. Duryodhana felt that Bhima's transgressions against the Kauravas were increasing by the day, and he constantly made fun of their weaknesses. He was worried that seeing the subdued response of the Kauravas, other Pandavas might start behaving similarly soon.

Bhima was gluttonous with an elephant's diet; he could never resist food. So Duryodhana devised a plan and called the Pandavas for a picnic and feast near the river. He poisoned Bhima's food, which made him unconscious. Then, while his brothers kept the rest of the Pandavas busy, he and a couple of other Kauravas tied up the unconscious Bhima and threw him into a river with poisonous snakes. There was no way he could live through this ordeal.

Most amazingly, as luck would have it, the snakes' poison—instead of killing Bhima—neutralised the poison that had been fed to him. Bhima had a fantastic encounter with the serpents who took him to their King, but that is another story. In a nutshell, Bhima escaped the ordeal and returned stronger than ever.

Meanwhile, very confident with what he had accomplished, Duryodhana told the rest of the Pandavas that Bhima had already gone home. When they all reached home, they did not find Bhima. They thought he may have stopped over somewhere on the way back, and they waited for him to return. Soon, not seeing Bhima coming back, they started to get worried. Search parties were sent out to find him but returned without success. Kunti was inconsolable, and the Pandavas were devastated.

Almost eight days later, Bhima walked back into Hastinapur, hale and hearty. The last thing he remembered was having a great meal at the picnic and then the exciting experiences in *Naga Loka*. The Pandavas suspected Duryodhana was responsible for all this but could not be sure. Vidur guided them not to make too much fuss on this issue since they were politically weak. So they decided to keep quiet. However, animosity between the Kauravas and the Pandavas increased dramatically after this incident.

Duryodhana was amazed at Bhima's return. How could Bhima escape such a foolproof scheme? It was impossible. He was unsure of what Bhima had told his brothers about what had happened that day. But since nobody seemed to be saying anything about it, he decided to behave normally, as if nothing had happened. But he felt uneasy. Maybe everybody knew everything, but nobody was talking about the incident. Could they be plotting behind his back to get revenge?

From then on, Duryodhana became very cautious in his dealings with the Pandavas or any of their supporters. Both Kunti (mother of the Pandavas) and Gandhari (mother of the Kauravas) saw these increasing tensions and felt deeply concerned about the kingdom's future. Gandhari was also aware that something wrong could have happened during the picnic. But she desperately wanted to believe that Duryodhana had not done anything wrong, and instead, a natural accident had occurred. Maybe Bhima had told Duryodhana that he was going home but had slipped into the river. Her mind continuously made up such scenarios, and she fervently prayed for the relationship between the brothers to improve. But in reality, the seeds for a lifetime of mistrust and hatred were sown, finally resulting in that fateful day of the dice game.

After this incident, though fights between the brothers continued, life went on relatively peacefully as they grew up together. The relationship even started to look as though it was improving. Even Duryodhana tried his best, at least outwardly, to make it seem that there was no animosity from his side. He knew in his heart that he would get even with them at the right time. He realised there was no benefit in demonstrating hostility openly. He was being ably guided by Shakuni, who was the only person he trusted. His father was blind and too weak, and even though Duryodhana knew he loved him, he was sure Dhritarastra would not stand up for him at the right time. As his Uncle Shakuni had told him repeatedly that to reach the throne of Hastinapur, Duryodhana needed to take matters into his own hands and not depend on his father or the other senior people in the court. They were either too weak or were fundamentally biased against him.

Chapter Five

Battle for Kinship

The senior courtiers and their gurus proposed to the King that since he was just a regent in place of King Pandu, they had to consider both the Pandavas and Kauravas equally to choose the next King of Hastinapur. Further, they told the King that given this reality, Yudhishthira, the eldest among all brothers, was the best choice for the throne. Additionally, from a capability point of view, he had the best attitude and aptitude to lead Hastinapur. As Duryodhana expected, his weak father fell for such arguments and declared Yudhishthira heir to the throne.

This incident was a big blow to Duryodhana. He was convinced that everybody in the world was indeed against him and went into deep despair. Why could his father not behave like a king? He had all the power, and his decisions were binding on everyone, but he chose to act like a true blind man! The courtiers were blatantly biased, and his father moved mindlessly under their influence. Even his mother wanted him to accept this reality and make peace with the situation. Duryodhana lost all hope and started thinking it was better to die than be ruled by Yudhishthira. As always, at this very low point in his life, only his Uncle Shakuni stood by him and told him not to lose heart. So, he gave up on everyone around him, and his uncle became his main reason for remaining alive.

His uncle was indeed a genius. He had already thought of an intricate plan, anticipating all these events. Duryodhana felt deeply indebted to Shakuni for believing in him and supporting him in these most challenging times of his life. His uncle comforted him, "Dear nephew, I have always told you never to let external forces bring you down. I know you will be the King of Hastinapur, come what may! I have not returned to my home all these years just to be by your side and ensure this. I always knew that the political forces of Hastinapur would never allow you to be King. But I have a singular purpose: to have you installed on this throne of Hastinapur, and I will make it happen. So do not let these small hindrances bring you down."

Duryodhana was thankful for Shakuni's support but did not understand what he could do in this situation. He responded despondently, "Uncle, I thank you from the bottom of my heart for all your love and support, and I also know that you are the only one in this palace who truly cares for me. But now, Father has already announced Yudhishthira as the crown prince. My father is only a regent waiting to hand over the throne to the real King, Yudhishthira. I don't know why my father behaves like this. He has all the power in the world, but he gets caught up in the arguments of the courtiers. I thought he would have built his internal strength all these years, and then he would get me my due. But he has failed me. I really don't have any hope. I don't know how you can ask me to be still hopeful. I don't see any solution."

Shakuni smiled and said, "My dear nephew, I have not been wasting these years doing nothing. I had foreseen many years ago that this situation could come about. I know your father well, and I was quite confident that the courtiers would prevail upon him. So, I devised a plan to get us out of this situation. Let me tell you what we need to do." Then Shakuni explained to Duryodhana an intricate plan by which they would get rid of Yudhishthira as the crown prince and all the Pandavas, including his bête noire Bhima, once and for all.

Duryodhana listened carefully, slowly grasping the master plan that his uncle was unveiling. First, they would celebrate Yudhishthira's becoming the crown prince. And then Duryodhana, as a mark of respect, would get a new palace made for the Pandavas in Vanavrata and present it to him. But the twist in the plot was that the whole palace would be made of lacquer. Lacquer catches fire very quickly. Shakuni had a very trustworthy architect for constructing such a palace. Then, at the right time—when the Pandavas were asleep—the palace would catch fire, resulting in the death of the Pandavas and their mother, Kunti. This incident would seem like an unfortunate accident, and after some days of mourning, the King would have to declare a new crown prince, and then he would be the obvious choice.

The plan sounded simple, but Duryodhana was worried as the Pandavas had somehow escaped the most intricate plans he had laid out in the past, like the one he had made to get rid of Bhima many years earlier. But Duryodhana had anyway resigned himself to the worst possibility, so this action plan seemed better than killing himself. Moreover, there was a good chance of this plan succeeding. So, he decided to go along with it.

Duryodhana's approach towards Yudhishthira changed. This surprised everybody. He was suddenly delighted that Yudhishthira had been proclaimed crown prince. Moreover, he publicly committed to building a new palace for the Pandavas to commemorate Yudhishthira's crowning. His mother and his aunt, Kunti, were amazed at the transformation. They found it hard to believe, but they went along, hoping their prayers had come true and everything was real.

Even the Pandavas were amazed at the change in Duryodhana's approach, but they were cautious, as they were never sure of Duryodhana's real intentions. Still, they were happy since Yudhishthira had been declared the crown prince. But Vidur warned them to be very careful in all their dealings with Duryodhana. He was suspicious of the palace that Duryodhana was building for the Pandavas, and he advised Yudhishthira to be extremely careful and keep his eyes and ears open. After some detective work, he seemed to have gotten a whiff of the game Shakuni was playing, and he passed that information on to the Pandavas.

The Pandavas moved to Vanavrata to the new palace constructed specially for them with great fanfare. They knew something was fishy and were very vigilant. In the new palace, Bhima never slept at night, and as a result, Duryodhana was unable to put his plan into action. His henchman and his most trusted ally in Vanavrata, Purochana, waited night after night unsuccessfully. He finally decided to poison the Pandavas instead. His wife served the poisoned food to the Pandavas. But, sensing something was wrong, Bhima ate all the food himself. Poison was not a problem for him because he had become immune to it after he had survived the childhood incident involving *Kalakoot* poison when Duryodhana had thrown him in the river.

The Pandavas dropped to the floor and acted as though they were poisoned and unconscious. Purochana was delighted as he thought his plan had worked. He and his sons started to drink and make merry. Soon, they got drunk and slept. Meanwhile, the Pandavas got up, set the palace on fire, and escaped. The charred bodies of Purochana, his wife, and their sons were discovered the next day, and people thought it was the Pandavas and their mother, Kunti.

Duryodhana was overjoyed when he got the news of the death of the Pandavas, but he was careful to express deep sorrow in public. Inside, he was euphoric. Finally, his uncle's plans had borne fruit. It was clear that only his Uncle Shakuni cared about his future. Why else would he leave his own family and stay in a foreign land for so long and help him execute these intense plans? Only he was concerned about making Duryodhana the King. While he knew his father wanted him to be the King, he did not have the will to execute it. He was more concerned about keeping the courtiers happy. His Uncle Shakuni was the only person he could depend on fully to take care of his interests.

Duryodhana went through the motions of the mourning period, grieving over the loss of his brothers. He knew that people like Vidur and many courtiers felt he was somehow responsible for this unfortunate incident, but there was no way they could prove it. Shakuni had planned this coup well, and there was no way anybody could connect the dots of this incident to him. Once he was declared heir to the throne, and it sank into all these people that the Pandavas were really dead and not coming back, they would all run to curry favour with him. He now knew the time had finally come when he would get what was genuinely due to him.

Dhritarashtra was also happy inside, though his mournful cries were the loudest. "How can I live without my very gentle nephews? Hastinapur has lost its most capable crown prince. Why did God not take me before taking the lives of my fair nephews?" he lamented, and the entire city of Hastinapur mourned with him. Duryodhana participated fully in mourning, but he watched Vidur's behaviour closely and felt something was amiss. The wily fox knew something more than he did, but he let that pass; soon, the kingdom would be his, and Vidur would ultimately cease to matter.

Did he feel sorry for what he had done? Not at all. Did people feel sorry for what he had gone through right from the time of his birth? No, nobody ever supported him for what was really due to him. The Pandavas had always eclipsed his life. The courtiers, especially Vidur, continued to plot against his success right under the nose of his spineless father. His mother was mortally afraid of confrontation, always asking him to make peace with the Pandavas. His teachers never gave him due appreciation for his great mastery over the mace; instead, they always extolled Arjuna's skill in archery and the wisdom of Yudhishthir. All these forces were aligned against him and working to undermine him, but he was committed to overcoming them and fighting hard for what was rightfully his.

In all these endeavours, he always had his Uncle Shakuni supporting him. Further, he had the support of his hundred brothers, specifically Dushashana, who was next in line and very close to him. Karna, his dear friend, had also stood by him in tough times. Given the current circumstances, he was convinced these were the best steps he could have taken. If Vidur could ask for him to be killed as a child based on some arcane omens, then what he had done now was absolutely right. As his uncle always said, it is a dog-eat-dog world. External forces could bring him down forever if he did not take his future into his own hands. He was thankful he had finally taken the required decisive action.

Soon, the period of mourning was over. Hastinapur had to have an heir to the throne, and who would be better than Duryodhana? The time which he had waited for all these years had finally arrived. His uncle's vision became a reality, and he was declared the crown prince. But his good days were short-lived.

Chapter Six

The Dead Come Back to Life

The Pandavas remained underground for many months, moving from place to place in disguise. During their wanderings, they landed at the *swayamvar* for Draupadi, the princess of the kingdom of Panchal. Arjuna won Draupadi's hand and she later became the wife of all five brothers.

After this, the Pandavas resurfaced and returned to Hastinapur with a beautiful wife. Duryodhana could not believe his plan had failed. But then he remembered Vidur's behaviour when the news of the Lakshyagrah incident had come; he was not as disturbed as expected. He suspected Vidur had helped the Pandavas escape. But that was just conjecture. It did not matter how they escaped. The burning issue was that they were back in town, which had its ramifications. The question of the crown prince was again back on the table as Yudhishthira returned. His father, now, had a problem on his hands. An erstwhile crown prince assumed to be dead had come back to life, but there was already a newly declared crown prince; a choice had to be made.

Duryodhana knew that Yudhishthira was a pacifist. So if his father just maintained the status quo and made no changes, Yudhishthira would eventually accept his fate, and life would go on. But as usual, his father became a target of the pressures of the courtiers who told him that he would have to do something for Yudhishthira. They first tried to convince him to rename Yudhishthira as the crown prince because he was more popular with the masses, but Dhritarashtra would have none of that. So, finally, Bhishma convinced him that the kingdom should be split into two parts to meet the aspirations of both princes. This solution was the final decision.

Duryodhana was not happy with this compromise, as he believed that splitting one of the largest empires in the country only served to weaken it, but there seemed to be no way out. Once again, fate had dealt him a blow despite all the planning he'd done with his uncle. But he was happy when his father gave him the current capital of Hastinapur and the surrounding more populated territories, which made Yudhishthira the King of Khandavaprastha, the most undeveloped part of the kingdom. It was a forest dominated by the Nagas.

So, Duryodhana remained the Crown Prince of Hastinapur and started to consolidate his power. His Uncle Shakuni, his most trusted friend Karna, and his brother Dushashna assisted him in this work. The Pandavas, led by Krishna, went to Khandavprastha and built their new capital at Indraprastha. They toiled to clear the forests and set up their new palace. With the help of a local Asura architect, Mayasura, whose life Arjuna had spared, a beautiful palace was raised in Indraprastha. It had a central hall called the Maya Sabha, which had a very well-polished floor, giving one a feeling of walking over water. It also had actual water in the middle, but it was so still that it looked just like the rest of the floor. It was indeed a palace of illusions. Duryodhana heard all these stories, and his jealousy was aroused. He could not believe the rate at which the population of Indraprastha was growing. He knew many well-to-do families of Hastinapur had decided to shift base to Indraprastha, seeing the economic fortunes of that city and surrounding area rise. He was getting worried.

Meanwhile, Narada, the celestial travelling sage, came to Indraprastha and appreciated the city's meteoric rise and how well the kingdom was managed. He proposed that Yudhisthira should undertake the *Rajasuya Yagna*. This *yagna* would spread Yudhisthira's power over many lands. It was a very intense, long-drawn, and costly sacrifice, but the victorious King would ultimately become a true emperor. Few kings attempted this feat, and even fewer succeeded, like Raja Harishchandra and Lord Rama.

Yudhisthira was not very keen and did not want to wage war in many territories. In those days, a mighty king in eastern India, Jarasandha, was supported by the neighbouring kings Kansa and Chedi. When Krishna was based near Mathura long before, he had been constantly at war with Jarasandha, but no clear victor emerged. Finally, tired of the constant battle, Krishna vacated Mathura with his entire kingdom and shifted to Dwarka, the westernmost tip of India. That is why Krishna was also called *Ranchod*, i.e., who ran away from battlefield. Krishna did not want his subjects to suffer because of this constant battle. He was okay if he got a derogatory name for his actions. Doing the *Rajasuya Yagna* would also mean taking on a formidable foe like Jarasandha.

Yudhisthira had no such ambitions for war and expansion. But Narada told him that this *yagna* was essential for his father's soul, which was stuck in the land of the dead. This sacrifice was needed for it to go to *devlok*. Based on this input, Yudhisthira, the dutiful son, felt he needed to help his father and agreed to conduct the *Rajasuya Yagna*. The brothers aligned many kingdoms that accepted Yudhishthira as the emperor without a fight. Some resisted, and wars were fought to establish the Pandavas' superiority. The most crucial battle was with the invincible Jarasandha, Krishna's long-standing foe.

Jarasandha had an interesting birth story, which made him very difficult to kill. Bheema finally beat him in hand-to-hand combat guided by Krishna's strategy. And so, Yudhisthira's *Rajasuya Yagna* was a resounding success. All the kings who had accepted Yudhishthira as their emperor were invited to Indraprastha for the final ceremony. The Kauravas, being part of the family, were also invited. And so, Duryodhana saw Indraprastha in all its opulence, which he had only heard about so far.

He was amazed at the Pandavas' progress in such a short time. So many people had settled in Indraprastha, and the city was humming with life. He was even more amazed at the palace and its quality; it boasted a new design and looked far superior to the palace in Hastinapur. His cousins had done well for themselves. They treated him well and took good care of his brothers. But as he went through the motions of his visit, he was burning with jealousy. He could see how much the Pandavas had gotten ahead of him in just a few years. Yudhisthira was now an emperor and many kings accepted his suzerainty. This disturbed Duryodhan no end. The Pandavas had become too powerful, and he was sure they would take over Hastinapur as soon as his father died. They only considered the Kauravas extended family out of regard for their old father. They knew he had made active plans to have them killed, and they would look for revenge at the right time.

Additionally, during this visit, a disturbing and humiliating incident occurred with Duryodhana. This was why he was looking so expectantly at the dice about to be rolled by Yudhishthira. As Duryodhana had walked across the floor of the Maya Sabha, where he marvelled at how the floor gave him a feeling of walking on water, he accidentally stepped into the part that was actually water. He was startled and shocked as he fell in and got drenched.

Arjuna and Bhima were standing at some distance and could not help but laugh after seeing his startled face. But the most painful part of the experience was that his sister-in-law Draupadi and her maids were looking on from the women's section higher up, and he heard them laugh. The deepest cut was the comment he overheard his sister-in-law make, which landed like a burning arrow in his heart. "The blind son of a blind father." He was infuriated and swore he would make her pay for this comment when the right time came.

Chapter Seven

The Revenge

Duryodhana left the palace with this incident deeply etched into his mind. Initially, he had not been happy about the division of the immense empire and had been contemplating how the empire could be reunited in the long run. But after his visit, seeing the increasing glory of the Pandavas, he knew he had to act fast to bring Indraprastha back under his rule and teach a lesson to the Pandavas and Draupadi.

As usual, he looked to Uncle Shakuni for advice. He was surprised that his uncle already had a solution for him. His uncle's wily mind never ceased to amaze him. Shakuni said to him, "Dear nephew, you underestimate your uncle... do you think I have taken this division of Hastinapur lying down? Not at all. It is a temporary settlement and will remain this way only over my dead body! I am committed to getting you your entire kingdom, not just a part of it. I did not talk about this earlier, as I wanted you to come to this conclusion yourself, which I am glad you have. These are matters of kingdom and power. Today, these kingdoms are tied together as your father is alive, and the Pandavas respect his views. But, as you rightly know, they are ambitious and want to take the entire kingdom after your father's death. If they were not so ambitious, why do you think they decided to conduct the *Rajasuya Yagna*?"

He continued, "As you have seen, they have built such a massive palace and well-sized city quickly. You have seen the power Yudhishthira has accumulated through the *Rajasuya Yagna*. Their size and the scope of their ambition will only increase with time. The Pandavas also believe that Yudhisthira is the true King of Hastinapur, and his position as the crown prince has been wrongly usurped by you. They also know you had something to do with the fire in Varnavrata. So they're just biding their time before they come to claim the entire kingdom."

Shakuni added, "Dear nephew, this world of power and politics is ruthless. Finally, only one person is the King, and that person's future generations rule; the rest all fall by the wayside. So you should act before them while your father is still alive." Duryodhana understood what his uncle said. He was right. He had to act now before it was too late. The Pandavas were already very powerful, and they could decide to take Hastinapur any day. Did he want the Kuru clan to be lost to obscurity forever? But how could he precipitate a situation while his father was alive to take over Indraprastha? His father would never agree to attack Indraprastha. So he looked expectantly towards his uncle for a solution. He asked, "While I fully agree with your analysis of the situation, uncle, what are we to do? The Pandavas have even defeated Jarasandha. They seem quite unbeatable. So many kings have accepted Yudhishthira as their emperor."

Shakuni replied, "Dear Duryodhana, all battles are not won on the battlefield. One needs to mould the situation to suit one's strengths and push for victory; that is the mark of a great leader. I have a plan we can implement as soon as you are ready. You just need to invite the Pandavas for a game of dice. Do it as soon as you can." Duryodhana was flabbergasted. "A game of dice! You must be joking, uncle! I need to wage war with them before they become too powerful, and here you are asking me to extend a hand in friendship?" He never understood his uncle's ways, but he knew that his devious mind had something cooking. Shakuni said, "My dear nephew, you always think in a straight line, much like the entire Kuru clan… but, as I said before, wars are won in many ways and not necessarily on the battlefield. Is it not better if you can win a war without bloodshed?" Duryodhana had to agree. He was now all ears to what his uncle had to say.

Shakuni continued, "Once you call the Pandavas for a friendly match, I intend to target Yudhishthira's weakness for this game. You know my skill with it, and I will make sure you win at the right times—you, Karna, and Dushasana must goad him to play more rounds till we get something substantial out of him. If we script this well, I am sure we could get the Pandavas to stake their entire kingdom, and then I will ensure your victory in getting the same." Duryodhana was amazed at the simplicity of the idea—no bloodshed—and at the same time, the entire Indraprastha would come to him in a friendly game of dice.

As Duryodhana watched the last dice roll, he saw how well the sequence of events had played out, precisely as his uncle had predicted. In the previous few rolls, he had won the entire kingdom of Indraprastha and the slavery of all the brothers for life. But this roll of the dice was important to him. He had hotly bristled at the humiliation his smart-mouthed sister-in-law had heaped on him. He knew she looked down upon him and felt that all five of her husbands were superior to him.

The comment she had made in Indraprastha in front of her maids burned in him; it was time for payback. He had goaded Yudhishthira to up the stakes to bet Draupadi, their wife, and as a wager, agreed to give back all that he had won till now if Duryodhana lost. Even before the dice hit the floor, he knew the outcome. He had even thought of his next steps after he won. He would call Draupadi, who would now be a slave to him, and have her dispatched to the slave quarters where she belonged. This would happen publicly in front of the entire court of Hastinapur. The haughty lady would be taught a lesson she truly deserved, Duryodhana thought smugly as he watched Yudhithira throw the dice on the floor.

The dice fell on the floor, and Yudhishthira's face fell; he could not believe chance would play so much against him. He had not won a single round for a long time and had lost everything, including his freedom. And on the last roll of the dice, he had lost his wife. He regretted his move immediately, but now there was no going back. Duryodhana was exultant. He had given the Pandavas their most crushing defeat ever. He immediately asked for Draupadi to be brought into the courtroom. He wanted to inform her of the defeat of her husbands in the game of dice and that she was now his slave. She was no longer a queen and needed to be in the servants' quarters, not the Queen's quarters.

He dispatched a servant to go and get her immediately. The servant left and soon returned, announcing Draupadi was not ready to come and that she had questions to ask the court about the validity of her ownership by Duryodhana. Duryodhana was visibly angry and sent the servant back to tell Draupadi to come and ask the questions herself, in the court. The servant made a second attempt but got the same response. Duryodhana was furious and asked his younger brother, Dushashana, to get Draupadi. He instructed that if she was not willing to come herself, she should be dragged forcibly to the courtroom.

The Pandavas looked on helplessly. Dushasana tried to convince Draupadi to come to the courtroom. Draupadi told him that this was the time of her menstrual cycle, and so she was not allowed to go out to any public place. Furthermore, she was dressed inappropriately due to her condition. Dushasana was in no mood to listen to these arguments. Draupadi again raised the question that if her husband had first staked himself and lost, he had no legal standing to stake her. Dushasana told her that she had better come to the court and ask questions, and if she disagreed, he would have to drag her there physically. Draupadi disagreed. So Dushasana dragged her to the courtroom by her hair.

She did not lose her wits in the courtroom and continued questioning Duryodhana's right over her. She brought out many legal points, which infuriated Duryodhana even more. He got so angry that he shouted that since she was his slave, she was at his mercy, and he could do what he liked with her. Then, in a fit of rage, he ordered that she be disrobed publicly for her impertinence to her master. The Pandavas were incensed but could do nothing. Bhima vowed to kill Duryodhana one day for this action. Only one of the Kaurava brothers, Vikarna, third in line among the Kauravas, spoke up against the act. He warned Duryodhana against this act, saying that he and the entire Kuru clan would have to bear the brunt of this sin. But Duryodhana and Karna silenced him.

Finally, Duryodhana ordered Dushasana to remove Draupadi's clothes. Dushasana obediently started to do as his elder brother asked. But as the *cheer haran* started,

Draupadi began praying to Lord Krishna to protect her modesty and respect. Surprisingly, even as Dushasana pulled the cloth fervently, it peeled away endlessly, collecting into a pile on the ground. And yet, Draupadi was still clad in the fabric. Nobody could understand what was going on.

Dushashna kept pulling till he was so tired that he fell to the ground. The whole court went silent, shocked at what had just happened before them. Then, Draupadi angrily raised pertinent questions about *dharma* in the court. The entire assemblage hung its head in shame, unable to give any respectable answer as to how this situation came to be.

Draupadi, now extremely angry, was about to curse the entire Kaurava clan when Gandhari intervened and forced Dhritrashtra to correct all the wrongs that had happened that day. Dhritrashtra quickly intervened, realising that things had gone awry that day. Most importantly, being scared of the power of the curse of a pure woman, he offered Draupadi three boons. The first two boons Draupadi asked for were the freedom of the Pandavas and the return of their weapons and kingdom, which Dhritrashtra immediately granted. On being offered a third boon, she said she could only take two as a Kshatriya woman, and asking for more things would be greedy of her. The immediate drama ended here, only to begin again at a later date.

Chapter Eight

Was this Fated or Destined?

The critical question in the above drama is whether the *cheer haran* of Draupadi, the most unfortunate event, could be considered a natural outcome stemming from all the characters' past. In other words, was it destined to happen? It's essential to understand the conditions under which this event occurred. This incident occurred in the court of one of the largest kingdoms on Earth. Highly educated and wise people like Bhishma, Dronacharaya, and Kripacharya, among many others, were present in the court. They all watched this abominable act occur right in front of their eyes while they debated its legality. Since the Pandavas had lost their freedom, the question was: could they technically stake claim to Draupadi? And if, in reality, the Pandavas had become the slaves of Duryodhana and the Kauravas, then was not Draupadi automatically their slave? And so the legal debate went on in endless circles.

The biggest question is whether all the past forces had aligned naturally for this incident, starting from Duryodhana's birth, upbringing, relationship with the Pandavas, and finally, his experienced (or imagined) humiliation in Indraprastha. But one could go back much earlier, even before Duryodhana's birth. For example, the unfortunate situation that led his father, Dhritarashtra, to give up the throne in favour of his younger brother Pandu while still harbouring a desire to bring the kingdom back to his family. This hidden desire was implanted deeply in his son Duryodhana right from birth.

We could go back even further to the ambitions of Satyavati, Dhritrashtra's grandmother, who forced her daughters-in-law, Ambika and Ambalika, to have Niyoga with Vyasa after Vichtravirya's death to produce viable heirs to the throne of Hastinapur. Vyasa was born dark-complexioned, and many years of penance had made his looks very rugged. Ambika was so afraid of Ved Vyas that she closed her eyes when she was intimate with him, and as a result, Dhritrashtra was born blind. Ved Vyas had foretold Satyavati that the child would be born blind immediately after the act, given Ambika's behaviour. In this fashion, all actions will have an infinite chain of cause and effect going into the long past.

Returning to Duryodhana, all his actions must be viewed through the lens of acceptable levels of the morality of those times. Jealous princes in those days went to great lengths to remove others from their path in pursuit of the throne, which was quite a normal aspect of palace politics. History could easily be rewritten by those who took the throne. Those removed from the path could be branded as evil, and those who ruled would be seen as just and godlike. The history of Hastinapur, and maybe even present-day India, could have been very different if the Kauravas had won rather than the Pandavas. Today, nobody in their sane mind would name their child Duryodhana in India as they commonly use Arjuna, Krishna, etc. The name has developed a very negative image, representing the ultimate villain.

At the same time, interestingly, there is a temple, Poruvazhy Peruviruthy Malanada, in Kerala, devoted to Duryodhana where they see him as a God and play the drum thrice a day to honour him according to a 5,500-year-old ritual. They also celebrate a big annual festival in March, attended by thousands of people.

Returning to the story, we wonder whether Duryodhana was destined to commit this act. While all the historical forces were working on his mind, he sought continuous advice from his Uncle Shakuni. What else could be expected from a person whose parents were either born blind or had consciously decided to blindfold themselves? The pain of his father, who could not attain the throne, was deeply embedded in him. All the forces were blindly pushing him towards this moment of revenge and the war of Kurukshetra.

Past forces play a critical role in shaping the future. Let's take the example of Shakuni. Shakuni had a dramatic past. Many years ago, his kingdom Gandhara had been defeated by Bhishma, who led the army on behalf of Hastinapur. The King's hundred sons were captured and thrown into a cell. Bhishma fed them a tiny amount daily; the idea was to starve them to death. The brothers knew that there was no chance of all of them surviving. So, they decided they would give all the food to Shakuni, who they believed had the cunning to carry out the revenge for all of them. Bhishma expected all of them to die due to starvation. But Shakuni survived due to this strategy, and he took a vow to destroy the Kuru clan to avenge the humiliation and disgrace of his brothers and father. So, he played on the jealousy between the Kauravas and the Pandavas to achieve this result. He was extremely cunning and skilled in the game of dice, and he used these abilities to bring about the Battle of Kurukshetra and the destruction of the entire Kuru clan.

Shakuni also wanted to avenge the insult doled out by Bhishma when he had proposed that Gandhari, his sister, be married to Dhritarashtra, a blind man. At that time, his sister had agreed, knowing fully well that if she did not accept the marriage proposal, the humiliation of Bhishma and Hastinapur would bring about many serious consequences for Gandhara. Therefore, Shakuni worked on fuelling the hatred between the Pandavas and Kauravas, knowing that it would escalate to a full-fledged civil war one day. He found an easy target in the volatile Duryodhana, whom he used as a tool to destroy Hastinapur. As he plotted these plans, the only person he feared was Lord Krishna, the only one who matched—and possibly exceeded—his intelligence. Krishna was also a shrewd diplomat and a great statesman.

So, even Shakuni was deeply influenced by his experiences and created a destructive weapon out of Duryodhana. We can say Duryodhana was almost helplessly moving towards this abominable act, controlled and managed by Shakuni.

In short, all forces of the past—both internal and external, playing on Duryodhana—brought him to this situation where he tried to execute the disrobing of Draupadi in public. Could he be blamed for the same? It seems pretty insane not to blame Duryodhana for such a dastardly act. But we can only blame someone if we believe there was any free will in the individual to have done otherwise. If Duryodhana were just an automaton playing back the various programmes installed in him like a robot, could we actually blame him? It would be like blaming a computer for executing all the programmes fed into it.

With all the hate and anger pent up inside him and his habit of throwing tantrums and getting his way throughout his life, he was set up to do what he did. He could not digest Draupadi questioning him in front of the entire assembly. He had expected her to be broken and crying at the turn of events and not question the legitimacy of his victory and the legality of his actions, that too publicly. This sparked his anger to a different level until he was in such a rage that he lost all reason and ended up doing the unthinkable.

We feel we are executing our "free will" as we make various decisions in life and choose different courses of action. For example, we refer to this situation in the following fashion: we decided to follow path A when we actually wanted to follow path B. Of course, there is no going back in time to test what we could or could not have done; the only reality is what we did. However, even if we found a way of going back in time, remembering that we had lived through this before (with the knowledge of the decisions we had made and their consequences), then we are not the same person who made a choice the first time. In fact, with all this added knowledge, a very different person is making a choice the second time around.

Either way, this situation is theoretical because going back in time is impossible. So, while what is done is done, we can only imagine what we could have done otherwise, which is an illusion. Most actions happen almost like an automaton based on what we have been programmed to do. This hypothesis is valid unless we can say that we have some ability in the current moment to diverge from the forces of the past. We will take up this train of thought later in this book.

Before that, let's examine Karna's history, which also had a bearing on that fateful day, as he had a long-harboured grudge against Draupadi. Karna was present during her *swayamvara*, where she married Arjuna. He had also participated in the competition for Draupadi's hand. None of the princes could lift the bow kept there for the competition. But then Karna walked in and tried—and lo and behold! He could easily lift the bow.

Draupadi realised that Karna could actually win the competition. So she suddenly stood up and said, "I will not marry a *suta* (a low caste)." Karna quietly bowed out of the competition for Draupadi's hand. But he always carried the grudge of the insult.

The big question is: why did Draupadi raise this point in the first place? She was a broad-minded woman. The idea of the *swayamvara* is to let the best man win. She was not one to break away from the tradition, so why did she say or do this? The truth is that Draupadi herself is a pawn in the hands of the big cycle of fate and is also fulfilling her destiny. She was not born of a normal womb; she was instead a gift of the sacrificial fire to her father, King Drupada. Her father, the King of Panchala, had once been defeated in battle by Dronacharya with the help of his able student, Arjuna. He felt severely humiliated and vowed to take revenge.

He knew he could not directly take on the might of Drona and Arjuna together, so he had conducted a big sacrificial *yagna* to help him avenge the humiliation. A son and daughter emerged as twins from the great *yagna*. The son was Drishtadyumna, who killed Drona during the Battle of Kurukshetra. The daughter was Draupadi, who became one of the fundamental causes of the rift between the Pandavas and Kauravas, which led to the great war of Mahabharata. Draupadi's role during the *swayamvara* was to choose Arjuna. Her key objective was to marry Arjuna and then create a split between the

Pandavas and Kauravas. Drona would be duty-bound to support the Kauravas, and as a result, Arjuna and Drona would be in opposite camps, with Drupada on the same side as Arjuna.

Only Arjuna was supposed to be able to perform the task set in the *swayamwara*. It was designed to be that way to bring Arjuna out of hiding. So Draupadi was surprised to see Karna lift the bow, and she knew that if she did not act immediately, Karna would go on and win the competition before Arjuna even tried. So she used the first excuse that came to her mind to get out of the situation and ensure that she and Arjuna would get married.

The rift between Drona and Drupada also has a fascinating story connected to it. Both Drona and Drupada studied together under one teacher, becoming great friends. They became so close that Drupada, a prince of the Panchal kingdom, promised to give half his kingdom to Drona. Later, by the time Drupada became King, Drona had gone into extreme poverty and could not even feed his family. He came to Drupada asking for help. He asked for half the kingdom as Drupada had promised. Drupada, realising the big difference in their stature, refused to acknowledge their friendship and shunned him, calling him a beggar.

Drona was deeply hurt and vowed to take revenge on Drupada. He got a job as a tutor of the Pandavas and attacked the kingdom of Panchal with the help of Arjuna and the Pandavas. He defeated Drupada and had him brought before him in chains. Then, he freed Drupada and gave him half the kingdom extracting his revenge. This sequence of events left Drupada feeling humiliated and this sparked the next series of events where he started to plot the death of Drona.

So, all actions by all actors in the Mahabharata have a historical perspective that one cannot ignore. Specific instances in isolation look pretty crazy, but new perspectives emerge with a broader view extending into the past. It becomes obvious why certain people behaved in particular ways, however bizarre it may look to an onlooker. In Hindu philosophy, this constant cycle of cause and effect is called the cycle of *Karma*. One is not able to escape one's karmic past. Our past impressions, samskaras, and conditioning push us to the destined action like dogs choicelessly chasing a bone thrown in any direction.

When we see the sequence of events in its entirety, we realise that nobody in that moment of the *cheer haran* in Dhritrashtra's court was there without a purpose. All past forces were unceasingly pushing everyone consciously or unconsciously towards their actions. Of course, the actions of one person impact those of another, and due to this, new and unexpected situations always pop up. But everybody is almost bound to do what they finally do. Could they have done anything differently? Well, that's just conjecture, and as discussed before, there was no going back in time to check this out. Since time travel to the past is impossible, we did what we could and could not have done otherwise. So, in a way, are we just playing out a larger script but experiencing an illusion of "free will" as we progress down our predestined path? In other words, was the *cheer haran* of Draupadi inevitable and had been written into her and Duryodhana's destiny long before they were born? Possibly, it was already written at the time of the universe's formation!

Part II

Yudhishthira

"A person often meets his destiny on the road he took to avoid it."

– Jean de La Fontaine

Chapter Nine

Anguish in Victory

He walked around the battlefield littered with bodies, flies buzzing around the corpses, and the pungent smell of blood and rotting flesh. Young men and older, in all shapes and sizes—some of whom he could even recognise as friends and relatives—all now lay inert and immobile, never to return to their loved ones. How difficult it was to give birth to a person and take care and groom them, and how easy it was to snuff life out. It was hard to imagine how hundreds of thousands had perished in just 18 days. As he stood and looked around at the carnage, a deep sadness overcame him. He knew this sorrow was so intense that it would be impossible for him to escape its shadow for the rest of his life. It would hover around him every day of his life in the coming years, like a ghostly spirit, reminding him of what he had brought to bear on this Earth.

He could hear the wailing of the widows who came to the battlefield looking for their husbands, some carrying small children on their backs, as there was no one to leave them with at home. Every time someone found the body of their loved one, there were loud wails.

Each shrill cry seemed like a knife plunged straight into his heart.

This situation, coupled with the heat of the afternoon sun, was making his head swirl—he felt he was just about to collapse on the spot. All this did not seem real, and he fervently hoped it could be a bad dream. But he did not even dare to pinch himself to confirm, as he was afraid it would all indeed be true. That would be just too painful to feel. It was safer to remain in this half-dreamlike state, numbing his mind and moving around like a zombie.

He wanted to wail out loud to release the immense burden on his heart, but that would not be appropriate. He and his brothers had just won a massive battle that had lasted 18 days. He was the king of the victorious side—then why this despair? He felt he was more a victim of his circumstances than a victor. He knew that the guilt of this devastating battle hung on his shoulders, but he felt more a victim of all the forces that had led him to this spot. How could he, the one they called Dharmaraj, be the cause of such devastation? As he looked hopelessly at the pain and misery around him, the question grew in his mind: Was there any justice in this outcome? Had he ended up in this position today out of his own choice? His mind naturally slipped back to his childhood.

Chapter Ten

An Idyllic Childhood in the Forest

Yudhishthira spent much of his childhood in the forest with his parents and later with his siblings. He knew his father, Pandu, had been a king who had left the throne of his own volition. This sacrifice was a penance for some wrongdoing during his reign. The misconduct had not happened knowingly, but Pandu, a very righteous person, had decided to take this call. Pandu had given up his kingdom to his blind brother Dhritarashtra and retired to the forest with his family. Yudhishtra had been personally impressed by his father's righteous behaviour. It was not necessary for Pandu, who had been more a victim of the situation, to take on such an immense penance.

His father had been hunting in the forest and saw some movement in the bush. He thought it was a deer and shot at it. In reality, it was a Brahmin and his wife who had been involved in an intimate act, which the king misjudged to be a deer and ended up killing the Brahmin instead. At the death of her husband, his dejected wife self-immolated on her husband's pyre and cursed the king that he would die if he ever had intercourse with a woman. There was also a bizarre twist to the tale. The Brahmin and his wife had taken on the form of a pair of deer to have intercourse in the open. They reverted to their human state only when the Brahmin was hit with the arrow. How was his father to know he was not shooting a deer but a human being?

But Pandu was a righteous man, and he knew that killing a Brahmin, however bizarre the circumstance, was a big crime, and he had to atone for it. So, while he had the curse to contend with, which was a significant enough punishment, he decided to abdicate his throne and head for the forests with his two wives, Kunti and Madri. It was something genuinely commendable for such a powerful king to do. His father upheld the highest values, especially as an all-powerful king, with every possible excuse to disown the act given the circumstances, which left a deep impression on Yudhishthira.

Given the story of this curse, he knew that he could not be the natural son of his father, or else his father would have been dead by now. While he was still young, his mother had told him that he was the son of Lord Yama, the God of death and justice. She was afraid that lest he hear of this from some other source, projected in a very wrong way, it would be better if she broke the news herself and did it the right way.

She had explained to him how, at a very young age, she had received a boon from Sage Durvasa that she could have a child of any of the Gods just by uttering a mantra. He was her first child when she invoked Yama. Whenever she talked to him about his being the first child, her eyes drooped, and her voice had some sadness. He could not understand this emotional reaction. Was she unhappy he was her firstborn? But nothing in her other actions showed that she was unhappy with him.

Kunti was extremely proud of her son, the epitome of humility and righteousness, always deferring to what she had to say, ready to sacrifice his happiness for what his family or society needed. He was an ideal son in many ways, peace-loving and compassionate. So, why did his mother's words falter when she explained his birth? It was only much later in life that he realised there was much more to the story than his mother had communicated. He was, in reality, not her first son, but that is another story.

Yudhishthira spent quite an idyllic period with his parents in the forest. Life was simple and without the glamour and political intrigues of a palace. This was an ideal place to learn from sages and enjoy time with his parents. If only life had continued in that place forever, Yudhishthira would have been only too happy. These first 16 years of his life were probably his best. His mother had two more sons using the mantra at her husband's request. The second son was Bhima, born to Lord Vayu; that is why he was so strong and powerful. His third brother was Arjuna, born of Lord Indra.

His stepmother Madri, Pandu's second wife, was remorseful, as she did not have children. So, Pandu requested Kunti to teach the mantra to Madri. Kunti taught her the same mantra but with the commitment that she would only use it once. Madri cleverly invoked the mantra for the Ashwin Kumaras, and as a result, the twins Nakul and Sahadev were born to her. These were the five Pandavas, the sons of Pandu.

Yudhishthira had seen and heard of his father's righteous behaviour since childhood. Additionally, his mother had drilled into him his birth story as the son of the God of Dharma (Yama is known as the God of both Death and Dharma). So, the highest level of ethical behaviour was always expected from him. Since his life began in the forest, he did not know what he missed of the pleasures in the palace; he only knew these humble surroundings. In reality, most children long for the attention and love of their parents and those around them. Yudhishthira got this love and attention in abundance, and it was one of the most important inputs into his character, which resulted in him being less demanding and wanting. Yes, he had four siblings, but there were three elders, their father Pandu, and his two wives, Kunti and Madri, who had a lot of time on their hands to take care of them.

This ratio worked much better than what the Kauravas, his cousins, got. A hundred of them were born in a hundred days, and they had their father and mother primarily and, of course, the numerous servants in the palace. But for a child, the love and attention of a father or mother mean much more than a hundred servants. So, in all probability, the Kauravas struggled for attention, making them more grasping and demanding.

As Yudhishthira stood on the battlefield that day, he tried to find reasons why the Kauravas had behaved the way they did. What was the need for this war? What was the reason for Duryodhana's unreasonable behaviour? Why did he (Yudhishthira) agree with Krishna to move forward with this battle? All these questions pounded on his mind, again and again. He had to finally accept that what had to happen had happened, and one could now only look back and build different narratives to explain it.

Gandhari, Duryodhana's mother, had been pregnant much earlier than Kunti, but Yudhishthira was born earlier due to a quirk of fate. All these realities put even more pressure on the Kauravas. They were used to the luxuries of the palace and had some exposure to the politics and power games played in the courtroom as they grew up. On the other hand, the Pandavas in the forest got their parents' focused love and attention and exposure to great sages and seers who imparted wisdom of a different type.

For Yudhishthira specifically, all these realities, coupled with the continuous input from his mother on his being the natural son of the God of Dharma, put him on an irreversible path of lifelong righteousness. He would follow the right path, even if it meant personal suffering or distress for himself or his near and dear ones. The rest of his life was a run-through of this script.

Could he have done anything differently along the way that would have averted this crazy war with all the pain it brought? He was not sure. Despite being so righteous and truthful, he could not reconcile how he had landed in this position today on the battlefield. Everything had happened logically, step by step, culminating in this *Dharma Yuddh*, as Krishna portrayed. How could he explain the victory of *dharma* to these wailing widows around him? He and his army had killed their teachers, cousins, uncles, and the court elders who had guided them through their childhood. All for this kingdom! Was it really worth it?

Yes, he had all the logic to explain why this war was necessary. He could recount all their efforts to subvert the battle and how Duryodhana had rejected their peace proposals until war was the only option. They had been ready to take only five villages in a remote corner of the kingdom to avert war, but even that was unacceptable to Duryodhana.

But would these logical arguments soothe these wailing women? Would it bring back the dead father of their children? What was done was done. Yudhishthira had no sense of victory; instead, he had a hollow feeling of defeat. His whole life devoted to truth and righteousness was now a big question mark. He was not even sure of what was right and wrong anymore. He wanted to go back to the forest where he had grown up. He had never enjoyed these trappings of power and the intricacies of palace politics anyway.

Chapter Eleven

The Return to the Palace

Everybody said he would make the best king for Hastinapur, which only increased the jealousy of his cousins, the Kauravas. Personally, he would have preferred to let Duryodhana have the throne right from the beginning, which would have sorted out many of the issues that ultimately caused this highly devastating battle. But all the courtiers and wise people were convinced he would make the better king. In reality, he had been a reluctant king throughout. Why was Krishna so keen to establish him as the King of Hastinapur? Even people like Bhishma and Drona, his enemies in this battle, wanted him to be the king—why? Why were they setting this narrative for him? If they had only let him be, things would have been simpler. Had this narrative set him up? Did he have the free will to walk away from it? He did not believe so.

His mind slipped back to more memories of his younger years. While the first 16 years of his life were probably the best, the sixteenth year changed everything. His poor father, struggling for so many years under the Brahmin's curse, made a mistake in a moment of weakness. It happened when the five brothers and Kunti had gone out into the forest. Pandu could not help himself becoming intimate with Madri, his younger wife. He passed away due to the curse. Madri was so overcome with remorse that she jumped into her husband's funeral pyre, unable to forgive herself for being the cause of his death. Now, the five young brothers and their mother, Kunti, were left alone in the world to fend for themselves in the forest. When Dhritarashtra learnt about this situation, he immediately asked Kunti and the Pandavas to return to the palace. Their mother agreed, realising the futility of raising five children alone in the forest.

Initially, Yudhishthira and his brothers had been excited to go and live in the palace. They were also happy to have a hundred more new playmates in the Kauravas. But this excitement was short-lived. Soon, they realised that the situation in the palace was not as simple as they had anticipated. The Kauravas, specifically Duryodhana, were highly displeased with their presence in the palace. He made every attempt to undermine the Pandavas. Yudhishthira, who was used to the simple ways of the forest, had never experienced this level of hatefulness and deviousness. The more he tried to be friendly and reach out to the Kauravas, the more they did everything they could to remove them from the palace. The atmosphere was always charged with palpable negative energy.

Gandhari and Kunti tried their best to make the cousins' relationship work without much success.

The animosity was further fuelled in the school they studied at. Everything became a severe, almost warlike competition. Yudhishthira today felt he had been naïve not to realise that all that rivalry would someday result in such a big war. Duryodhana always knew that this war was on the anvil—and even talked about it—but Yudhishthira, forever an idealist, wanted to believe they would outgrow this childhood rivalry. But he could not have been more wrong.

Was this horrible war written back in the days of their childhood? Was he just a pawn in the hands of time, living out his conditioning without choice? He had always tried to do the right thing in every moment throughout his life. This value was very important to him. Today, he wanted to understand whether he had participated in this war out of his personal choice or it was his destiny, which he could never have escaped. He felt a strong urge to ascertain this conclusively. He realised the importance of doing so because it would decide how the pain and grief the war had wrought on the larger kingdom would sit on his shoulders.

He did not want to answer this question quickly or too easily because he knew that his devious ego would like to walk away from the blame of the moment. Any good, socially acceptable argument would do. He had to be careful not to fall into that trap. He was, after all, Dharmaraj, the ultimate upholder of truth and justice. More than anyone else, he had to be one hundred per cent sure before accepting any argument.

Everything seemed unreal as he moved around in a zombie-like state on the battlefield. His mind was continuously slipping between the present and the past; the distinctions were blurred, if any at all. All the past and present seemed to be happening right now, and it wasn't easy to separate the real from the imagination. His mind swung to the time in the palace after the return from the forest.

The situation in the palace was grim for the young Pandavas. Far from having new friends, they had some serious enemies now. Duryodhana, goaded by Shakuni, always had some crazy plans up his sleeve to get rid of the Pandavas. He hated Bhima the most. Bhima was huge and very strong and terrorised the Kaurava brothers in many ways. But Duryodhana feared Arjuna more, who was getting more skilled in archery by the day. He would be a formidable foe in battle. Whenever he saw Arjuna practising, Duryodhana felt he was practising for a war against the Kauravas.

While Yudhishthira always tried to be friendly and respectful with everyone, Duryodhana saw him as a weakling. Yudhishthira was acutely aware of all these feelings that Duryodhana had. Why couldn't they all just look beyond limited realities, see the greater benefit in coexisting, and build an even stronger Hastinapur with happy and prosperous subjects? As a true idealist, he felt these animosities would fade away as they all grew up. He constantly stressed the possibility and benefits of coexisting, even though some viewpoints would always differ.

But, in reality, things deteriorated further. The deepest trough in the relationship came when Bhima disappeared after the picnic that Duryodhana invited them to. When he returned a few days later, Bhima told a strange tale of what had happened to him. All fingers seemed to point towards foul play from Duryodhana and the Kauravas. The Pandavas wanted to investigate the matter thoroughly, but their mother and Uncle Vidur asked them to lie low and not raise the issue much. They asked the Pandavas to take all these disturbing incidents in their stride as they feared further retaliation if certain things came out in the open. Yudhishthira, always dutiful and respectful of the elders, followed their advice. Incidents like these and how the elders reacted to them made Yudhishthira long for the old forest life, which was more straightforward and truthful. The palace had a lot of pleasures and comforts, but it was a treacherous place to be. After this incident, the Pandavas were doubly vigilant.

Today, as he contemplated his past, he tried to see where he could have gone wrong, which resulted in his experiencing a day like this. He had always wanted reconciliation with the Kauravas and not to fight them. But Duryodhana's extreme approach always confounded him.

Chapter Twelve

Kingship and Politics

Yudhishtra's flawless character and deep wisdom impressed all people, especially the courtiers and ministers. They were convinced he would make a great king, leading Hastinapur to heights. Therefore, they all pressured Dhritarashtra to install Yudhishtra as the crown prince. Yudhishtra knew of the feelings among the brothers and dreaded taking on this role. He knew well that this would take the rivalry between the Pandavas and Kauravas to another level. But could he turn down the offer?

It was the well-considered decision of the king, ministers, and the wise men of the kingdom. He had to respect that decision. He was surprised at the way Duryodhana seemed to react to the situation. He seemed happy at this announcement. At that time, everything seemed unreal and hard to believe. Maybe Duryodhana reconciled to his fate once his father made this decision. Perhaps he had decided to respect that decision and bury the hatchet, thought the idealistic Yudhishthira. Now, he wanted to please Duryodhana, who seemed to behave exceptionally well.

Duryodhana was not only happy with this announcement but also went ahead and constructed a unique palace for the Pandavas in Varnavrata to commemorate Yudhishthira's announcement as the crown prince. Yudhishthira could not believe his ears but went along with the celebratory mood of the moment. He did not want to do something that would anger Duryodhana more than anything else. To make him happy, he even agreed to go and stay in Varnavrata.

His wise Uncle Vidur warned him not to fall for Duryodhana's antics and to keep his eyes and ears open for all kinds of games he could play. But for now, Yudhishthira wanted to believe that something had changed. He had only experienced hatred and anger from Duryodhana throughout his life. But, for the first time, the situation in the palace looked different. It was too good to be true! Yudhishthira was actually happier about improving the equation with his cousins than about the fact that he had become the crown prince.

He could see that his mother and aunt Gandhari were also amazed at the turn of events. They wanted this to be true, so he played along. As the Pandavas left for Varnavrata, Vidur again gave hints to Yudhishthira that something was wrong in the palace they were going to stay in. Yudhishthira valued any input given to him, especially if it came from a highly respected and wise individual like Vidur. As the Pandavas reached Varnavrata, Vidur sent another person who dug a tunnel from the palace to a riverbank, gave the Pandavas the key to the trapdoor to the tunnel, and then left. Yudhishthira realised that Vidur would never go to such pains until he was confident that something would happen soon.

For added safety, he asked Bhima to be awake every night. When the Pandavas got a whiff of Purochana's plan to poison them, Bhima, who was immune to poison, ate all the food. Then, the Pandavas lay down, pretending to be unconscious and slowly dying of poison.

Purochana and his family, comprising his four sons and his wife, entered and, on surveying the scene, felt their plan had succeeded. They decided to drink and make merry before setting the palace on fire and obliterating all the evidence. However, they ended up drinking too much and fell asleep. That's when the Pandavas got up, set the palace on fire, and escaped through the trap door to the river where Vidur had asked a boatman to be present to take them to safety but to keep them incognito.

Yudhishthira could not believe the turn of events. Vidur helped them so much. Purochana and his family were the same size as the Pandava family; everything seemed too beautifully coordinated, as if everything had been preplanned. He had only learnt to do the right thing in life and had never cared about the outcome. That was in God's hands. Throughout his life, he had noticed that unexpected forces came to his aid and saved him from disastrous consequences. But, at the same time, his rigid adherence to his principles had led him and his family through quite a lot of pain and tribulations from time to time. Yudhishthira knew that while his family read everything as a gain or loss based on different actions, he read the world differently. His purpose was just to do what was right and not care about the consequences. He would graciously accept whatever came as his due and continue to act in a just and righteous way.

Even today, as he stood on the battlefield, it was being seen by all those around him as his greatest victory. But for him, the situation was his worst defeat. Many people described this moment as the victory of good over evil, of *dharma* over *adharma*, so should he not be happy? Then why was he feeling so disoriented and disturbed? The women's wails on the battlefield were getting louder as more bodies were recognised. These sounds were echoing in his mind and drowning out all else.

Even if he believed this was a battle between *dharma* and *adharma*, was this a permanent victory of good over evil? He knew the answer only too well that this was not true and would never be true for any battle. There was nothing like a permanent victory of good over evil. These were just repeating cycles of pain, and unluckily, he had been the spearhead of this round. Today, he had the deaths of all these people on his conscience; it was a burden he had to bear.

But the burning question on his mind was whether he had created this war and this extensive carnage out of his own free will or not. He had many courtiers to guide him, and he always took a wider group of people to form a consensus on any crucial step. But of course, as the king, the final decision had always been his. His brothers had no choice but to follow his call to war as he was the eldest. Krishna was also an adviser whom he could have overruled. This decision was his. Could he have chosen otherwise? He could have said no to the battle, and many lives would have been spared. This was a difficult question to answer. Yudhishthira's mind slipped back to the events that finally led to the war.

Chapter Thirteen

Was this Divine Will?

After roaming in the forest for many years following the Lakshagrah incident, Panchali (Draupadi) joined them as their wife. King Dhritarashtra became aware that they were alive and called them back to the palace. Duryodhana was shocked to see that the Pandavas had managed to escape. When it was time for the King to choose between the two Crown Princes, Bhishma advised Dhritarashtra to split the empire so that both Yudhishthira and Duryodhana could be appeased. Dhritrashtra followed Bhishma's advice and gave Duryodhana Hastinapur and the Pandavas the eastern, less developed part of the kingdom called Khandavaprastha.

What irked the Pandavas was that no investigation was carried out into the Lakshagrah incident. Instead, they had been sent to the harsh forest area of Khandavaprastha. The Pandavas had always been treated this way. While everyone knew Duryodhana's devious machinations, he was somehow always protected. Nobody had the guts to raise these questions to his face. He was rude, aggressive, and violent, and nobody wanted to get on his wrong side. Even his parents were scared of pushing him towards what they felt was right. This one fact was probably the key reason that Duryodhana turned out the way he did. Things could have been different if he had been raised with a firm hand.

The five Pandavas had a similar upbringing and life together, but each was poles apart in nature and character. While highly loyal to the family, Bhima had a short fuse and could lose his temper over small things and get aggressive and violent, especially when he felt the family was being wronged somehow. On the other hand, Arjuna was highly focused on whatever task he set himself. He always tried to perfect himself in whatever art or skill he wanted to learn. This keen focus and commitment to perfection was visible through the fantastic skills he had honed in archery. And then, Yudhishthira himself was so different from his brothers due to his righteousness. Even the twins Nakul and Sahadev, born of the same mother on the same day, were very different in many ways.

His brother's decisions and actions were often influenced by their internal makeup more than environmental influences. But does the internal makeup only determine a person's choice? If yes, how could one choose something that was determined literally from birth? Even if we suppose one is just a combination of a God-given internal makeup starting from birth and external or environmental factors like parental upbringing, etc., then how can anyone be held accountable for what they do?

This line of thinking disturbed Yudhishthira, as this seemed to point to a place of zero accountability for all actions. If this was true, he and Duryodhana were not responsible for their actions. Everything was predestined and without choice. It had happened as expected, without the exercise of any free will by any of them. It meant that this dominance of *dharma* in his views, which he seemed so deeply concerned about, was meaningless. He was not deciding to act righteously and truthfully in all circumstances; rather, he was programmed to do so without any choice.

Even Krishna had told Arjuna that he was just a tool in the hands of the divine. So, he had to do his duty and leave the rest to God. The larger forces in the universe knew what was required, and sometimes, one became the tool of its implementation. However bad the current situation may seem were things happening for the best, as divine will would want it?

To Yudhishthira, it felt like he was an independent being with free will, making choices and deciding to do the right and just things at all times. Could that be an illusion? If yes, this would absolve him of all the consequences of his actions, like this devastating battle. But, if this absolved him of the responsibility of this battle and the people who had died, it would also absolve Duryodhana from the Lakshagrah incident or the *cheer haran* attempt on Draupadi. This line of thinking was going nowhere, he thought. He felt further depressed. But if this indeed was the reality, whether it depressed him or not, running away and hiding from it was not a solution.

Yudhishtira recollected that whenever he had been the king of a territory, that territory had prospered. Indraprastha, previously called Khandavprastha, a largely uninhabited forest area, flourished under his reign. The size and scale of success in Indraprastha had been so great that Yudhishtira could successfully carry out the *Rajasuya Yagna.*

He could not understand why a reluctant king like himself could achieve so much in such little time. Whatever his period of rule, wherever the subjects were—the kingdom had prospered beyond anyone's wildest dreams. Maybe the Gurus and courtiers saw something in him, so they pushed for his candidacy as the next king. Why was this so? What did they see in him? He could easily be defined as a reluctant king, yes— righteous and courteous but not very decisive—instead, consultative, i.e., listening to a broader group of people before deciding anything.

Of course, the courtiers would want a leader who listens to them, but few would prefer an impartial leader who would listen to all equally and not have favourites. People like Shakuni would want the leader to listen only to them. That is why he preferred Duryodhana, who could easily be manipulated and managed. People like Vidur and Bhishma would wish for a leader like himself, who was balanced, impartial, and committed to truth and justice in the face of all odds, even at the risk of a huge personal loss. But the proof of the pudding is in eating it. Finally, what kind of leadership paid off? The lands Yudhishthira governed prospered far more than anyone would imagine.

While he never felt any pride in this, it is possible that his way of working and governance had something to do with the kingdom's prosperity. His philosophy was to make a right and just decision and leave the rest to God. Whatever the outcome or result of the action, accept it as a gift from God. Sometimes, the gift was a success, as seen by the world, and sometimes it was a failure. But to him, all this was *prasada* from God.

If his presence as king benefited a larger group of people, he would endeavour to do that. He could be well-programmed to do this role, or he could be a being possessing free will, making the correct decisions that benefit everyone and hence be the right person for the role of a king. Whichever the case, getting him established on the throne was the right thing to do. He started to feel better as this line of thought built up in him. This is precisely the logic that Krishna had sold to him and all the kings who supported him, that *dharma* had to be victorious, and *adharma* had to be removed from the world. That is why this battle, the removal of the Kauravas, and the establishment of the Pandavas was essential.

But did that justify this war? Could Krishna, who was himself worshipped as none other than the supreme personality of God, be wrong? When he spoke to Arjuna, he convinced him to go to battle, saying that he was all-knowing, all-powerful, and the primary cause of action in all beings. He had set up this stage, and Arjuna was just a tool in his hand to conduct this action. Arjuna had been trained and developed for this very moment to act as a tool of the divine will. At that moment, the key goal was to wage war with all his might without thinking of victory or loss. Behave as a tool of God and a sacrifice for the greater good.

Yudhishthira felt that he had been trained for kingship in the same fashion, which was being put to use accordingly by the same divine will. He was just a tool of the divine to act in the way he had been trained since birth. This battle had been triggered by Krishna himself, who was extremely clear about the outcome. So why should he now feel bad as he stood on the battlefield, victorious and ready to begin a new era in the history of Hastinapur? The glory days of this kingdom were still ahead, and this is how Krishna had envisaged it.

This sounded like a much better narrative. The more he thought about the incidents that led to the war, the more he realised that the battle had been pushed ahead by none other than Krishna. Then, who was he to take responsibility for the same? He was just a pawn in the hands of the more significant forces. If Krishna were to be believed, all beings are just that—created by divine will to live in a specific fashion and fulfil their destinies. This thought calmed him and made him more accepting of the current reality.

But what worried him as he followed this line of thought was that if the principle of divine will was used to explain everything, then there was no judgement on anyone. Everyone did whatever they did without a choice and as an expression of divine will. This view absolved all, including Duryodhana, of the consequences of their actions. Somehow, Yudhishthira was not comfortable with this view. It made all the other life structures redundant, including his father, the God of Dharma's role. If everything was the action of divine will, who was the judge of *dharma* and *adharma*? Despite the rising confidence, this nugget of doubt troubled him. He felt envious of the guidance that Krishna gave Arjuna. He longed for the same advice. Who could rest his mind, which had gotten completely lost in this circle of 'free will or no free will,' *dharma* or *adharma*? Whom should he ask for help or clarification?

Chapter Fourteen

Yudhishthira's Dilemma

Krishna was the only one he could approach among all the people he knew. But at times, Yudhishthira felt Krishna did things that did not fall on the right side of *dharma*. Yes, Krishna always claimed to uphold *dharma*, but he asked him to tell a white lie to Drona on the battlefield that Ashwatthama was dead. Ashwatthama was the name of an elephant and also of Drona's son. Drona knew Yudhishthira would never lie, so he asked if Aswathama was dead. Yudhishthira confirmed that he was, knowing fully well that Drona was asking about his son. Still, he replied in the affirmative without mentioning that he was referring to the elephant named Ashwatama. Drona was shocked and went into a stupor, and the moment of weakness was used to kill him. All this was executed under Krishna's guidance.

For a person like Yudhishthira, who always stood for truth and righteousness under all circumstances, this attitude of Krishna was hard to condone. Unluckily, because of this deceit that Krishna enacted, he became the tool for Drona's death. Later, Krishna guided Bhima to break the rules of one-on-one combat with

Duryodhana and hit him on the thigh, which resulted in Duryodhana's death. While all these actions resulted in him and his family finally winning the battle, were they right? Even righteous Balrama, Krishna's elder brother, was very angry at how the rules were broken in the duel. These were crucial turning points in the battle, and deceit had been used by none other than Krishna, who was considered to be God by most.

Under the searing heat of the afternoon sun, surrounded by the stench of the corpses and the continuous wail of the widows, delirium overtook Yudhishthira again. The initial confidence generated through the argument of being a tool of divine will seemed like a shallow response to the starkness of the immediate reality. He could not walk away from his responsibility and blame everyone around him or any divine will for the situation. That went against whatever he had heard and learnt in his entire life. One had to take responsibility and do the right thing. And to do the right thing, one needs some free will. Had his father not taken responsibility for killing the sage, even though it had happened by mistake, and forsaken his kingdom? He could have easily said that this was the act of divine will and absolved himself.

For Yudhishthira to stand on this battlefield and absolve himself of all consequences of his actions would be equivalent to his father continuing to rule and live a normal life after killing the sage. This was impossible for a righteous person like himself to do. He knew what Krishna would say if he asked about this dilemma burning him from inside. He would say the same thing he told his younger brother, Arjuna, before the battle when he had lost heart and did not want to proceed. He would ask him to do his duty, not worry about the consequences of his actions, and leave those to God. Not far removed from his philosophy of doing the right thing moment to moment and accepting whatever came as a consequence—being happy even if it meant personal loss or pain. Yudhishthira himself had followed this philosophy all his life. However, there was a subtle difference between how Krishna executed this philosophy and how he did it.

This difference initially looked small, but when looked at deeply, a huge philosophical divide made Krishna and his approach stand at opposite poles. While he (Yudhisthira) would only be interested in the "means" being proper, he would never be concerned about the "end." On the other hand, Krishna's actions demonstrated that the "end" was more important than the "means." This thought never sat too well with Yudhishthira; he felt this was the root cause of his dilemma today. He was never in favour of the battle; he had wanted conciliation. He felt that Krishna had created the grounds for war through his dealings and actions. Krishna kept claiming that he wished for conciliation, but in reality, he wanted this battle to occur so that *dharma* would defeat *adharma* in a strong, clear, and conclusive manner. He almost let *adharma* build up to a peak, and then the war became imminent.

If he was God, as he claimed, and was truly omnipotent—could he not have made Duryodhana see reason and find some compromise? Yudhishthira felt he could have easily done so if he wanted. But Krishna wanted the destruction of *adharma* and not a compromise with it. This battle and all the pain it caused was an outcome of that need of Krishna. He had told Arjuna that it is his duty to come to Earth whenever there is a rise in *adharma*, and the sole purpose of his *avtaara* is to destroy *adharma*. The Pandavas were just the tool of this destruction. So, for Krishna, the end was more important, and the means were flexible. Once the war started, this "any means" to take him to the "right end" became evident and blatant.

The risk with such a philosophy, Yudhishthira felt, was that one needed to be confident of what the "right end" is. There had been many fanatics in the past, and many more would be born in the future who claim patronage under this philosophy, proposing that they definitely knew the "right end." They would continue to wreak havoc in the world using wrong means to achieve their imagined right end.

It was Krishna who had driven the Pandavas to battle. When they wanted to stop the war, as Arjuna had wished to drop his weapons at the beginning of the battle, Krishna roused them back to action. Today, the destruction Yudhishthira saw around him resulted from Krishna's insistence. During the war, when situations were very much in favour of the Kauravas, Krishna guided them to use deceit and break the rules of war to turn the situation in their favour until he achieved what he wanted. But how could he be sure that *dharma* resided on the side of the Pandavas, especially when they themselves were using deceit? Also, how could he explain this philosophy to the wailing widows? What had they and their young, innocent, fatherless children done to deserve this—would they see all this as *dharma*?

He knew that there were no easy answers to these questions. All the actions of deceit that resulted in victory in this battle would rankle him no end. Whether he had free will or not, Yudhishthira would go through life behaving and acting as though his actions came about through his own free will and he was responsible for them. He would continue to live and execute the principles of *dharma*, which he had learnt and established within himself throughout his life, but his past misdeeds would never be buried. This great battle had truly humbled him.

It was not a great victory but an opening to a period of deep self-reflection about what was truly right and wrong. The foundation of his life as the Dharmaraj was the ability to discern right from wrong. But today, he acknowledged that he was lost in making this distinction. It would require much more introspection before he would find solid ground again. He sighed and walked slowly back towards his camp, resigned to take on the duties and burdens of a king and, more importantly, the burden of all the confusion within his mind about what was right and wrong.

Part III

Krishna

"The future is completely open, and we are writing it moment to moment."

– Pema Chodron

Chapter Fifteen

Gandhari's Curse

He stood there looking at the ground. His inconsolable aunt stood near him, her tears refusing to stop. Initially, his aunt had not realised that he had come to meet her. She had been so overcome with grief that she had forgotten everything around her. It took some time for her to recognise that Krishna was standing there. She had a cloth tied to her eyes, which prevented her from seeing anything, but she had developed a unique sense of knowing who was in her presence. In deep grief, even this sense had dulled. As she realised it was Krishna standing before her, she experienced a surge of anger. This was the man who could have stopped this war but did not, so was he not directly to be blamed for the situation?

Her grief quickly transformed into rage towards this person who stood in front of her. He called himself a God, a supporter of *dharma*, and one who claimed to know the future. He was the root cause of the death of her hundred sons. If he had seen this coming, could he have not averted it? He had been the chief negotiator between the two sides, and most people on both sides greatly respected him. Preventing this war would have been child's play for him.

During the battle, she heard that Arjuna did not want to engage in this bloodshed and wanted to leave the battlefield. But it had been Krishna who had convinced him to stay on and fight. There had been so many opportunities to prevent this battle. But this man, or God as everyone believed, who now stood in front of her, had not allowed any of them to fructify. He had wanted this battle; he had wanted her sons dead.

She had lost all her sons—not one or two, but a hundred of them—in 18 days flat! Less than a month back, she had all her sons by her side and had been helping them prepare for this battle while taking care of their small needs. Now, they were all gone—strong, able-bodied men with long and productive lives in front of them. Luckily, she had tied this cloth to her eyes and could not see the dead bodies of her many sons. For sure, she would not have survived that sight.

But soon, her remorse was overridden with rage towards this person standing before her. Uncontrolled wrath rolled out from every pore in her body; she was beside herself with anger. Her voice was high-pitched and harsh as she spoke, "Should you not have averted this war with all your divine will and power? You were at the centre of all discussions, and everyone listened to you; could you not have shown some mercy instead of pushing this whole family to war? You wanted this war to happen all along, and you wanted my sons dead. You will never know the pain of a mother who has lost all her sons in a span of 18 days. Go ask your mother, who lost seven children at birth; I lost a hundred in ripe adulthood."

The more she spoke, the more her anger mounted. She expected Krishna to say something in response, but there was no response. Instead, through her blindfolded eyes, she felt there was just calm acceptance on the part of Krishna, no remorse, and no feeling of guilt. This sparked her anger to another level—what did he think of himself? How could he just destroy her family and be so calm and relaxed as if nothing had happened? He would only understand if he lost his own family.

By now, with her anger at its peak, she cursed him with all her heart and soul, "O mocking God, may you see the destruction of the Yadava clan right before your eyes. May the Yadavas fight among themselves and kill each other, much like you have made the *Kuruvansh* do today. May the cities and gold-laced palaces of your kingdom sink to the bottom of the sea. Let the pain, sadness, and gloom encompassing my family and kingdom today consume the Yadava clan. May the Yadavas kill each other and die out... May the Yadavas die out."

Everyone present, other than Krishna, was shocked. There was no way of taking a curse like this back. People moved in to calm her down, but Krishna motioned for them not to. He seemed very calm, almost accepting of the curse, as though he expected this to happen. He actually looked relieved that this moment had passed. Gandhari suddenly realised the weight of her words and started to cry as she collapsed to the floor. Her anger swiftly evaporated as though transported out of her body by each word she had just uttered.

As she sat sobbing on the ground, Krishna moved towards her and consoled her, "Mother, your curse will definitely take effect not only because of the meritorious life you have lived but also because of the larger play of things in the universe. You and your actions are just a small part of a bigger puzzle about which you and those in the audience here have no knowledge. But I am fully aware and was just waiting for this moment. Thank you for delivering the required curse on my clan. They will soon get what they fully deserve. So please don't feel bad about what you just did; rather, let's now work to give due respect to those who died on this battlefield and send them on their heavenly journey."

With this, Krishna calmly walked past the shocked audience without any trace of unhappiness or anger at the turn of events. He knew in his heart that the Yadavas were slowly becoming extremely powerful, especially under his protection. And the power was going to their heads. They had chosen wayward self-aggrandisement and focused only on increasing their pleasures instead of working for the betterment of society. The current situation was still not so bad, but

Krishna could clearly see how bad things would get long into the future. Gandhari's curse was a solution to that situation. He internally thanked her for taking the load of the destruction of his own race from him on her shoulders. Everything that happened was for a purpose; the universe knew what it was doing. One could say that however damaging to oneself the action looks in the moment; it is perfect and essential at that precise time. Nothing else should or would have happened.

Krishna could see all events from the past thousands of years and what was to come for the thousands of years ahead. However trivial or mundane it seemed, each event was happening for a purpose, the fruits to arrive in this lifetime or another. At the beginning of the war, he had pointed out to Arjuna that the difference between himself and others on the battlefield was this only, "Many a birth have I passed through, O Arjuna, and so have you. I know them all, but you know them not, O scorcher of foes." Through his awareness, he could enter into any detail, from a random thought entering a person's head to seeing things on a much broader level extending over thousands of years.

Chapter Sixteen

Destiny and Purpose

Krishna knew well there was nothing Gandhari or he could have done about the curse. Her sorrow was as valid as her anger, and this curse had to come. He could have explained many things to Gandhari, but it was no use at this time. She would never understand in this moment of sorrow. She would only comprehend things much later if he explained to her once her sorrow had subsided. She would, in all likelihood, ask him, "Whose purpose could it be to have my hundred sons killed and then the Yadava clan decimated?"

Arjuna had asked him the same question as he stood on the battlefield, confused about whether to participate in the battle. Krishna had explained logically and systematically why he should participate in the war. He also explained that it was not Arjuna's decision to participate in the battle at all; the larger forces of the universe decided that he had to fight this battle to achieve the critical purpose of the destruction of injustice on the planet. Meanwhile, Arjuna had to experience the entire dilemma, and the *Bhagavad* Gita had to be delivered by Krishna to him. All this was slated to happen.

Till the very last, Arjuna was doubtful and confused. It was then Krishna showed his real self. It was his huge and all-encompassing multidimensional form. All Gods were seen within him; fire blazed on all sides, and all living beings and nonliving things were part of him. All the past, present, and future were within him. Already, all the Kauravas were being killed by him as they rode into his ferocious mouth, but so was everybody else dying with time. Arjuna was afraid of what he saw; all things were being created, maintained, and destroyed continuously and unendingly. It was not as though he saw all this with his mortal eyes; his inner awareness saw and experienced it. He knew his physical eyes were incapable of grasping this dimension. Krishna's blessing allowed him to have this divine vision of the universe.

He realised that Krishna, whom he had seen as his friend, guide, and mentor, created and maintained the entire universe. Everything was Krishna's will, and all those who stood on the battlefield were just tools in his hands. In a universe like this, he was only to play his role, not worry about victory or defeat, giving his best in the moment and leaving the rest to God. Arjuna was truly convinced of this after experiencing Krishna's divine vision. He had been a fool to doubt Krishna. He was now committed to whatever action God wanted him to execute.

But Gandhari was not ready for this. Each person must psychologically be ready to grasp the entire reality.

Until this knowledge is fully absorbed, the illusion of our lives obfuscates reality, and the new vision has difficulty descending.

Krishna at no point guided Arjuna not to undertake action—on the contrary—Krishna told Arjuna that he needed to undertake all actions that came due to him and for which he had been trained and developed all his life. Krishna's message was of intense action: become one with the action but be detached from the consequence of actions. Accept the result of action as a *prasad,* and irrespective of a good or bad outcome, continue to act as per one's calling, doing the right thing for the greater good of the universe.

As per this view, all action is an offering to God, or better still, is to grasp the truth that God acts through oneself. We become tools in the hands of God or the larger Universal energy, which is conscious, aware, intelligent, and with a purpose. Often, we don't understand the larger purpose and get upset and angry as Gandhari did, but then, even the curse she had to give was necessary. Even in her anger, she was a tool in the hands of Krishna. Krishna had used Gandhari to deliver a curse unto himself! With time and the evolutionary process, people understand these things more clearly, and the spiritual path opens with incredible depth and width. And in a rare moment through the grace of God, one has a revelation, as Arjuna did, and all pieces fall into place.

But for Gandhari, there was only one script of her life, which she was deeply wedded to and running with. She felt confident about a single chain of events that led her to her current reality. She felt she was nothing but the accumulation of information about her past. She was the daughter of the King of Gandhara, and she was the wife of Dhritrashtra. She had received a boon to have a hundred sons, and these sons were born most mysteriously from a single pregnancy. All these facts, and many more, made her Gandhari, differentiating her from others. These were real physical things that had occurred, as she remembered them. They were a continuous cause-effect cycle. Whatever did not fit neatly in this cause-effect cycle was conveniently forgotten, and only the main well-connected pieces remained. In short, her reality was her limited memory of what had occurred.

None of the past was actually there in the current moment, only her limited memory of it. But she wholly owned her past. And that watertight rigid ownership was her ego, and she resisted any shake-up to her past information structure. The tighter she held on to the past, the more pain she experienced. She was in extreme pain from having lost all her hundred sons.

She could choose to break away from her current storyline, but that would take immense focus on being in the moment and distinguishing the Universal experiencer from the experienced storyline. This process would detach her from her limited storyline and make her realise she was none other than Krishna himself, just entrapped in a limited viewpoint. But instead, since her storyline was concrete, her destiny was equally solid. In a way, she was creating her own reality. But then, this was also her destiny and hence her purpose.

Chapter Seventeen

Time and the Experiencer of Time

Krishna knew that the flow of time was relative. He could slow down time to view one lifetime occurring in a thousand human years or speed it up and see many lifetimes just skip by in a few human moments. There was no absoluteness in the experience of time; the flow of time depended on the experiencer. Different creatures experienced different rates of flow of time. Calling any of these experiences authentic and the rest false was incorrect.

Krishna remembered how, in his current avatar, he had helped King Muchukunda achieve *moksha*. Muchukunda was a great king of the Ikshvaku dynasty during the *Satya Yuga*. He was a brilliant war strategist and fighter. During those times, the Devas and Asuras were constantly at war. At one point, the Devas were losing to the Asuras, and they asked King Muchukunda for help. The king obliged, and he ascended to *Deva Loka* (heaven) to fight on the side of the Devas. He threw himself into the task, fought without relief for a long time, and held the fort for the Devas.

Later, the Devas got Karthikeya to be their commander, and Indra approached Muchukunda to ask him for a boon for all the services rendered. Muchukunda asked permission to go back to his family and kingdom. Lord Indra unhappily told him that time flowed differently in *Deva Loka* than on Earth. A few years in *Deva Loka* are many centuries on Earth. Of course, Muchukunda's family and kingdom were long gone. He was otherwise happy to grant any boon other than granting *moksha*, for which he had no power. The king told Indra that he was exhausted from years of fighting and wanted to take a long, indefinite sleep from which no one would disturb him. Indra gave him a boon that he could sleep indefinitely, and if anyone disturbed him, the person would be burned to ashes. The king came down to Earth and went into a cave into a deep slumber. There, he slept for thousands of years.

More recently, in *Dvapara Yuga*, Krishna had been defending Mathura from Jarasandha, who had taken help from the Yavana King Kalayavan in his battle against Krishna. Kalayavan had boons from many Gods and was undefeatable. Krishna knew he could not fight him directly. But then, he remembered Muchukunda was sleeping in a cave and had the boon that would burn anyone who woke him up to ashes. So Krishna acted as if he was running away from Kalayavan, who started chasing him. He ran into the cave where Muchukunda was sleeping and hid in a corner. Kalayavan followed him in, saw a person (Muchukunda) sleeping, and thought it was Krishna. He kicked the person awake. Muchukunda got up after thousands of years and looked at Kalayavan, who was immediately burned to ashes. Krishna then guided Muchukunda on the path to *moksha*.

Muchukunda's story demonstrates how subjective time is. Different *lokas*, or planes of existence, have different timelines. We, as humans, can coordinate our actions because we are all aligned to a similar timeline, but that is not fixed or absolute in any sense. This is just one of the many timelines that exist.

As he walked towards his quarters after receiving the curse from Gandhari, Krishna thought of the flow of all the events that led to this. Unlike all the other people present, he could immediately see the connections stretching hundreds of years and lifetimes. Nothing here was happening by chance. Everything was a well-coordinated flow. **Interestingly, while everything looked destined to some and entirely occurring by chance to others, in reality, the situation was neither this nor that**. The human mind always thinks in black and white. The functioning of the universe is not so straightforward. The universe is not a preset machine with no possibility of change. It can change and play with options, but they are not exercised randomly or by chance; instead, they are conscious calls of the alive and self-aware universe. Within this fundamental reality, different illusions of time are subjectively experienced by different beings.

Krishna always referred to Universal consciousness as himself. He had explained to Arjuna, "Those who know me as unborn and beginningless, and as the Supreme Lord of the universe, they among mortals are free from illusion and released from all evils." With the exhalation of one breath of his, thousands of Brahmas or Universes are created, and with every inhalation, they all get sucked in and cease to exist, and this process goes on indefinitely. Brahma, the creator, has a day that equals 4.32 billion human years. One Brahma's lifetime of 100 years means an incredible 311.04 trillion human years, called the *maha kalpa*. So one can imagine that in one exhalation of Vishnu, hundreds of trillions of human years pass. This cycle of exhalation and inhalation is non-ending and eternal. That is why he referred to himself as eternal.

For a being existing in time, this reality is hard to imagine. Arjuna experienced himself being born, growing up, and reaching this point of the Battle of Kurukshetra. He also saw Krishna as his friend, who had travelled with him through time. But for Krishna, this particular time experience was one of the infinite illusions he had created for enjoyment or play. He is eternal, unchanging, never born, and never dying. That is his fundamental nature.

Chapter Eighteen

Krishna's Leela

Before the war, Krishna had been sensing the strengths and capabilities of the warriors coming to Kurukshetra to fight. As he went through this process, he came upon Barbarik, a great warrior. Barbarik was the son of Ghatotkach and grandson of Bhima. He had only three arrows, but he had the boon that he could fix all the targets he wanted to destroy when shooting the first arrow, and then the arrow would return to the quiver. Then, when shooting the second arrow, he could mark all the things he wanted saved, and finally, when he shot the third arrow, it would destroy all the things marked for destruction.

Krishna, disguised as a Brahmin, wanted to test him. He asked Barbarik to tie the leaves of the tree they were standing under. Barbarik agreed. Krishna secretly placed a leaf from the tree under his foot as Barbarik closed his eyes to meditate before shooting the arrow. The arrow marked all the leaves of the tree and started hovering around Krishna's leg. Krishna asked Barbarik why that was happening, and Barbarik replied that there must be a leaf below Krishna's feet. The moment Krishna removed his foot, the arrow also marked that leaf. Krishna realised the exceptional powers of Barbarik. Krishna asked him which side he wanted to fight from. Barbarik told him he had committed to his mother that he would fight from the losing side.

Krishna immediately realised that Barbarik should not fight. If he did, he would fight for the losing side, which would get stronger due to his presence, and start winning, forcing Barbarik to shift to the other side. This would go on indefinitely till only Barbarik was left standing. He raised this issue with Barbarik, and Barbarik realised what would happen if he participated in the battle. Krishna then asked Barbarik for his head as daan (donation) to prevent this situation. Barbarik agreed but asked that his head be placed at a point where he could see the entire battle of Kurukshetra. Krishna granted him the boon.

After the battle of Kurukshetra was over, there was a debate about who the main hero or the person responsible for the Pandava's victory was. Different warriors at that time claimed and believed they had been crucial to winning the battle. A proposal came up that everyone should go to the head of Barbarik and ask who truly won the war. Krishna, the Pandavas, and many warriors went to the head and asked this question. Barbarik replied that all he had seen was the Sudarshan Chakra revolving everywhere and cutting off the heads of all those who were killed. He could only see Krishna acting everywhere on the battlefield. Through the grace of God, Barbarik saw reality as it is, i.e., Krishna or Universal consciousness acting through many of its varied creations. All the creations are but his tools of action.

Arjuna is also one of Krishna's creations, and the experiencer within Arjuna is the same Universal consciousness or Krishna consciousness. So, for Krishna, Arjuna is another keyhole to reality for himself, like all other living beings. The only point to note is that when he experiences the world through Arjuna's being, he chooses to forget his true nature as Krishna or Universal consciousness. This situation is like in a dream, where we forget that we are in a dream because if we knew that we would not enjoy that experience as much.

Each conscious being has a different perspective on the same situation. For example, Duryodhana, Yudhishthira, and Gandhari had completely different perspectives on what transpired during the 18 days of the Battle of Kurukshetra. In reality, the experiencer of these illusions was none other than the same Universal consciousness or Krishna. Universal consciousness is the only thing alive and capable of experiencing anything in the universe. ***It is also the fabricator of what is being experienced***. Through its creations, it experiences multiple dimensions of its potentiality. Everything in this universe is conscious awareness, which takes different shapes and forms. It can experience and enjoy the illusion it has created while forgetting its true nature.

Since everything is this eternal consciousness, this physical body with its five senses is also the same consciousness condensed and used as an experiencing tool by its creation. Likewise, everything we experience outside is also an illusion created by consciousness, or one could call it a condensation of consciousness. So the experiencer and the experienced are one! This is what Barbarik saw – the observer and observed are one and the same.

But in our physical world, we see things differently. We experience duality, i.e., two things: the experiencer who experiences and the external world, which is experienced. Through experiencing itself, i.e., sensations within the body and those arriving from outside, we differentiate between what is the body and what is not. This process creates the illusion of *Maya*, and Krishna's *leela* begins. Universal consciousness forgets its true nature and starts to fragment reality as it becomes an individual.

Gandhari experienced in her subjective universe that she had a hundred sons born from her body. So she was attached to them and felt they were hers, while the Pandavas were born of another person and thus were not hers. It would be very challenging for her to buy the argument that there was one reality in the universe and everything, including herself, was Krishna, only she had just forgotten this. It was her myopic, inaccurate view of reality, that lead to all the pain. This is how her and Krishna's views of reality differed. But Krishna knew it would be no fun to be in a dream where one is aware that one is in a dream. So, this forgetting that Gandhari was experiencing was a part of his *leela*. What was happening was perfectly fine, as he had planned it to be.

The above logic would hold for everyone, not just Gandhari. The pain that Arjuna experienced when he lost Abhimanyu led him to avenge his son's death by killing Jayadratha the next day before sundown. Arjuna had experienced Krishna's *Vishwaroopa* avatar. Technically, he knew that the whole play was that of Krishna and that he was just an actor. All choices were Krishna's, and all outcomes were as he decided. Still, he felt deeply immersed in this duality and could not accept the truth that Abhimanyu's death was Krishna's decision. He experienced deep anguish and anger at what happened and reacted as such. So, the knowledge of this reality is not enough, and one falls back into the illusion despite having this knowledge.

Every individual needs to complete their cycle of *Karma*, and until that is over, they remain in the illusion of duality, experiencing all the pains and pleasures therein. The dream is Krishna's *leela*, which no ordinary human can escape. Only the deepest faith, love, devotion, and acceptance of His Will would lead the person out of this cycle of *Karma*, towards *moksha*, and out of the constant unending cycles of experienced time.

Chapter Nineteen

Infinite Timelines and Parallel Universes

Krishna experienced the larger reality, creating it as he wished from moment to moment. On one side, he was the Universal creator and experiencer of all the illusions; no individual self existed for him. On the other side, all his creations were his parts through whom he enjoyed the *Maya* or illusion that he had created. Time was an illusion he had created within the timeless but eternal moment.

Krishna recollected the time when Brahma had come to meet him many aeons ago. He wanted to expand Brahma's perspective of reality, so when the doorman told him that Brahma had come to meet him, he asked which Brahma it was. He knew this would create confusion in Brahma's mind, which Krishna would resolve in a unique way. The doorman returned with the answer from a perplexed Brahma that he was the four-headed Brahma. Krishna asked the doorman to usher him in.

As expected, Brahma arrived and immediately asked the question that Krishna was waiting for. Brahma asked, "Dear Lord, why did you enquire which Brahma had come to see you? Is there any other Brahma in this universe other than me?" Krishna smiled, closed his eyes, and went into deep meditation. As he meditated, many Brahmas started to arrive. These Brahmas had different numbers of heads. Some had ten, some 20, some one hundred, some one thousand, some one million, and some one hundred million. The number of faces was impossible to count.

Then, an innumerable number of Shivas and Indras arrived. Many Indras had hundreds of eyes on their bodies. When the four-headed Brahma, the creator of our universe, saw all this, he was bewildered. He realised his insignificance in the infinite diversity of the number of existing universes.

All the Brahmas and other Gods paid obeisances to Krishna and thanked him for giving them a chance to be with him. Krishna then asked them if they were okay and if there were any issues with demonic forces in their jurisdictions. The Brahmas replied there were none, and wherever they had such problems, Krishna himself had descended on the planet and brought the right balance towards righteousness.

As the four-headed Brahma saw the amazing vision of the variety of Gods and goddesses unfold in front of him, he realised something even more surprising. None of the visitors were aware of each other, nor could they interact with each other individually in any way. But all this was happening simultaneously! Only he (the four-headed Brahma) could see all of them, but they could not see anyone other than Krishna, and they all felt they were interacting with Krishna alone. After some time, Krishna bade farewell to the various Brahmas who left after offering due obeisances to him. The four-headed Brahma could not comprehend how such a thing was happening. He fell to the feet of the Lord, acknowledging that understanding the myriad dimensions of Krishna was beyond the reach of his mind, body, and words.

So, for Krishna, or the Universal consciousness, there are always multiple realities (or illusions) experienced all the time, but he experiences every small thing intensely—from a mere leaf falling from the tree to the most complex emotional experiences we can have; all are created and experienced by him. He becomes one with the leaf as he becomes one with Gandhari in her pain and grief. At the same time, he is one with Gandhari in the parallel universe, where she does not tie the cloth to her eyes. All this comes to him effortlessly. It is eternity enjoying its infinite dimensions and possibilities.

While Krishna was simultaneously experiencing parallel realities (or illusions) equally intensely, his only method of experiencing each of these illusions was through his creations like Gandhari or Arjuna. He became them and forgot his true infinite nature in a particular illusion. He experienced pain and joy through their characters. Rarely did he appear in his illusions as he did as Krishna. Even in his role as these avatars, he respected all the ground rules of the illusion. He respected Gandhari's grief at the loss of her hundred sons and Arjuna's despair at the beginning of the Battle of Kurukshetra. He was a mere charioteer for Arjuna during the war and gave his *Narayani Sena* to Duryodhana. He did not want to disturb the illusion fundamentally. Still, he wanted to provide his highest teachings through the discourse of the Bhagavad Gita and restore *Dharma* in his own illusion, which he effectively achieved.

Chapter Twenty

Cyclical Timelines within an Everlasting Eternity

Krishna had a firsthand experience of the many parallel universes, and most importantly, he remembered everything. Not only did he remember them, but he also experienced them all happening right now! The human mind works from moment to moment, but Krishna experienced the past, present, and future as all happening together. Much like a movie reel, we see screen by screen, but in reality, all the past, present, and future are already created and available for viewing. The creator of the movie knows the whole story. Similarly, our senses cannot see the entire film together, but Krishna or Universal consciousness can experience it in its entirety at the same time. Unlike a film director, Krishna not only remembers these experiences from his memory or knows the whole story, he also experiences them as happening simultaneously, i.e., all the past, present, and future happening all at once.

While this is very difficult for us to imagine, this is what it means to be beyond space and time; time stops moving, and all the past, present, and future occur together. This was the *Vishwaroopa darshan* that he (Krishna) had shown Arjuna. That *darshan* cannot happen through our normal sense structure. Arjuna was disturbed and confused by the entire experience and pleaded with Krishna to bring him back to his ordinary world experience. It was too much for him to absorb in one go.

Krishna remembered a lesson he had taught Hanuman in his earlier avatar as Ram in *Treta Yuga* to expose him to the unending cycling of events and experiences. When *Ram Rajya (dharma)* was established in Ayodhya, it was time for Ram to return to his abode, but his devotee Hanuman would not allow it. Yama, the God of death, often attempted to take away Ram's soul but was unsuccessful. Hanuman would always remain near Ram and not allow Yama to succeed. Ram realised the issue and knew his time to leave Earth had come, so he decided to trick Hanuman into leaving his side for some time. He dropped his ring through a crack in the floor, making it look like an accident. He then asked Hanuman to get him his ring. Hanuman immediately obliged. He had the power to shrink himself to a size smaller than a fly, which he did and promptly went after the ring.

The crack turned out to be surprisingly deep, and Hanuman went deeper and deeper. Finally, after a long time, he reached the lowest level in *Patala Loka*—the *Naga Loka*. Vasuki, the king of snakes, rules *Naga Loka*. Interestingly, Vasuki is the snake that hangs around Siva's neck. Vasuki asked Hanuman why he had come. Hanuman replied, "Lord Ram's ring has fallen through a hole that leads to this place. I have come in search of that." Vasuki agreed to take Hanuman to the ring. He took Hanuman to the centre of *Naga Loka*, where a mountain of rings was piled up. "You will surely find Rama's ring here," Vasuki said. Hanuman was surprised to see so many rings. But then he was shocked when he picked up ring after ring, and all were of Ram. He was confused and did not know what to do. He looked expectantly at Vasuki for guidance, as only he seemed to understand what was happening.

Vasuki explains to Hanuman, "This world goes through continuous cycles of time or *Kalpas*. Each *Kalpa* has a thousand cycles of the four *Yugas*: *Satya Yuga, Treta Yuga, Dvapara Yuga,* and *Kali Yuga*. In the second *Yuga, Treta Yuga*, Ram takes birth in Ayodhya. Then, one day, his ring falls into this world of the Nagas. A monkey comes searching for the ring, and Rama dies on Earth. All these rings testify that this has happened so many times. The mountain keeps growing as more rings fall. There is enough space here for many more rings of Rama."

In this fashion, Vasuki explained to Hanuman that it was time for Rama to die, and he should accept that. He further explained that the thousands of rings in the huge pile symbolised Lord Ram's numerous births. He concluded that thousands of Ramayanas took place and that there was enough space for more rings of Lord Ram, suggesting that Lord Ram will be born again and he will meet Hanuman again. He said that he collects these rings, keeps them, and awaits the arrival of Hanuman. Hanuman then realised that his Lord's incarnation in this life was ending, though there would continue to be numerous incarnations in the future. Further, he realised he had been tricked into leaving Rama's side, but now he had a deeper acceptance of what was to come. He then left *Naga Loka* to return to Ayodhya.

Krishna remembered Hanuman very fondly. He had been his dearest devotee in his Rama avatar. In his current avatar, Arjuna was equally dear to him. During the *Vishwaroopa darshan,* he had shown Arjun the past, present, and future together, which shocked Arjuna as he was used to living life one frame at a time. But Krishna is eternity, and all these unending cycles of illusions of time and space occur on this bed of timeless eternity. He knew all of them and enjoyed them experientially, being able to stand both within and outside them. Within these cycles of illusion as different beings, he chose to forget his eternal nature to enjoy the illusion frame by frame (in time). But he could also choose to stand outside and experience all the past, present, and future together, as he did in the *Vishwaroopa darshan.*

How would a being living in a single storyline or along one timeline describe parallel universes if they were exposed to, say, multiple parallel possible narratives of Mahabharata? Their senses would not allow them to experience these simultaneously since they experience everything sequentially, one frame at a time. They would naturally describe them as repetitive cycles, as though things seem to repeat themselves but with some variations. Krishna experiences everything simultaneously effortlessly; for him, all the pasts, presents, and futures are always occurring. For a being within the illusion, the past gets over and remains only as a memory; the present is only real. For Krishna, the present is very wide and all-encompassing, containing all the possible pasts, presents, and futures. For him, all possibilities remain alive. These stories are woven again and again by the various beings in time within this everlasting eternity, and this is the amazing quality of Krishna's *leela*!

Chapter Twenty One

Krishna's Dharma

Krishna always claimed that he had taken this incarnation to re-establish Dharma on earth. He tells Arjuna in no uncertain terms, "Whenever there is a decline in Dharma and an increase in sinfulness, O Arjuna, at that time I manifest myself on Earth." If this was so, then why did he make Yudhishthira, the epitome of truthfulness and *dharma*, tell a white lie to kill Guru Drona? Later, he guided Bhima to strike Duryodhana on the thigh, which was against the combat rules, to kill him. These actions seem quite counterintuitive. But then this is Krishna; through his contradictory actions, he propagated his teachings.

Krishna has a message for the world in these actions – *dharma* is conditioned by time, space, and circumstances. This was the time of the end of the *Dvapara Yuga*. Society had become very unethical by this time, and people's thoughts, words, and actions were far from consistent. They played with words, using them for their convenience. Through his actions, Krishna demonstrated that there are times when one should acknowledge that some people may play unfairly and must be dealt with accordingly. In other words, you may use means that may not be considered entirely fair, but the purpose is to achieve an end that upholds *dharma*.

Contrary to this, Yudhishthira would follow the rulebook almost unthinkingly. He would not question or break them, irrespective of whatever others were doing wrong around him. Despite Duryodhana's despicable behaviour, when he publicly tried to disrobe Draupadi, Yudhishthira kept quiet and did not act to prevent that from happening. He got caught up in legal arguments about whether he had the right to stop Duryodhana. The rulebook was more critical for him.

On the other hand, Duryodhana uses the rulebook for his own convenience, following it or dropping it whenever he wants. For him, *dharma* was flexible and could be twisted to support one's egoic needs. But Krishna is ready to break the rules and play necessary politics as long as the ends justify the means. His desired end was the destruction of *adharma* and the establishment of *dharma*.

On the eighteenth and last day of the Battle of Kurukshetra, Duryodhana, realising he was losing the battle, sat in deep meditation under the water in a lake. The Pandavas located him, and he challenged one of the Pandavas to a duel. If he were defeated, then he would acknowledge defeat. But if he won, he would be the final victor of the entire Battle of Kurukshetra. As usual, following the rule book (the principles of *Kshatriya dharma*), Yudhisthira took the bait, much to the dismay of his younger brothers.

While Yudhishthira agreed to this challenge, he was unaware of the source of Duryodhana's confidence. The previous night, his mother, Gandhari, realising that her sons were losing the war, told him to bathe in the lake and come to her without any clothes. Her idea was to remove her blindfold and look at him because she had a boon that whatever she saw would become solid as iron and indestructible. Realising something fishy was afoot, Krishna met Duryodhana as he walked to his mother's tent. Krishna chided him for not wearing any clothes and entering his mother's chambers. As a result, Duryodhana decided to cover his lower part below the waist up to the thigh. Gandhari opened her eyes, and his body turned invincible except for the thighs. Gandhari immediately realised that Krishna had again ensured that her son would be killed despite all her efforts.

It was decided that Bhima would fight Duryodhana, and the duel began. Soon, Bhima realised he could not hurt Duryodhana at all. He seemed invincible. The game's rules are that the opponent cannot hit below the waist in a mace fight. But Krishna hints to Bhima to do precisely that and reminds him of the oath he had taken in public: that he (Bhima) would break Duryodhana's thigh. During the *cheer haran*, Duryodhana bared his thigh and asked Draupadi to sit on his thigh. That is when Bhima took this public oath. This reminder ignited intense fury in Bhima, and he hit Duryodhana on his thigh with full force, which brought Duryodhana down and took him to his death. Here again, Krishna pushed Bhima to break the rules to ensure the victory of *dharma*. This action was necessary because Gandhari and Duryodhana played an unfair game, and without Krishna's intervention, *adharma* would have won. Krishna's message was clear: the ends justify the means.

Chapter Twenty-Two

Krishna's Contradictions

Krishna is a master of contradictions. Unlike his avatar as Rama in the Treta Yuga, where he set the example of living a life strictly based on ideals, , in *Dvapara Yuga*, he showed the world that he did not shy away from breaking the written rule when he could clearly see people breaking the rules and defended these actions by facetious arguments. Some of the rules he broke were a show of compassion in certain difficult situations. However, the key message was that intention is everything. He did not prescribe just playing with words to rationalise all sorts of actions, which was prevelant towards the end of *Dvapara Yuga*.

He had an unbelievable number of 16,108 wives. Here, Krishna demonstrated the ability to enjoy, and at the same time remain detached from these pleasures. As mentioned before, many of the actions were compassionate responses, appreciating the needs of the moment. He had freed 16,100 ladies from slavery after a battle with a demon. These women had nowhere to go as abducted enslaved women, and they knew their families would reject them if they went back. So, they all wanted to commit mass suicide. Krishna agreed to marry them and give them his name. Now, marrying them was not just a tick in the box. He needed to be able to provide each one of them with the love and support they required. He created so many replicas of himself and made time slow down so that each woman felt fulfilled. All his choices were practical and relevant to the reality (or illusion) that he existed in.

He was even ready to be called Ranchod (the one who ran away from battlefield) because that was a practical and suitable response when Jarasandha planned to attack Mathura, supported by several allies.

Jarasandha was the powerful ruler of Maghadha. He had taken a vow to kill Krishna since Krishna had killed his son-in-law, Kansa. He had attacked Mathura 17 times but failed, and now he was planning his largest attack, supported by his allies, for the eighteenth time. Krishna realised that after repulsing 17 previous attacks, the Yadavas were exhausted and incapable of taking on another attack by Jarasandha.

Jarasandha sent a message that he would not fight if Krishna and Balrama's heads were handed to him. The Yadavas refused to take the offer and were getting ready for battle. Krishna was against the war at that time. He proposed that they all leave the city and relocate to Dwarka. His grandfather Ugrasena pointed out that if Krishna ran away from the battle, he would forever be known as a coward or *Ranchod*, i.e., one who ran away from the battlefield. Krishna replied that he was not concerned if another name was given to him. "I already have many names; one more will not make any difference. Moreover, I am willing to sacrifice my reputation for saving my people and their lives," he said. A very practical and authentic response indeed!

Krishna was not foolhardy; he did not want to tinker with the basic fabric of the illusion he had created. He could have assumed superhuman powers and destroyed Jarasandha and his supporting allies. But then that would be breaking his creation's rules and physical laws. He used all the natural forces and emotions at the moment to achieve the required end. He never participated directly in the Battle of Kurukshetra himself. He respected the rules and laws of nature and played by them. He never granted superhuman powers to those he supported; all battles and actions had to be real and practical, not magical. The battle of *dharma* versus *adharma*, and the unequivocal victory of *dharma*, had to be real and not a fantasy.

Chapter Twenty-Three

Krishna, "I Set You Free."

Krishna could look into the future as he could look into the past. He could transcend the limits of space and time at His Will. The critical point is that while transcending all these limitations, he still seemed bound by the curse of Gandhari or needed to run away from Mathura and be called Ranchod. Further, he experienced multiple realities (or illusions) where other possibilities played out simultaneously. So, was he the creator of reality moment to moment, the primary experiencer and actor within all living beings, or was he just a spectator (and enjoyer) of various possibilities playing out without choice?

From the beginning, Krishna had made it clear to Arjuna that he would not directly participate in the Battle of Kurukshetra, i.e., not pick up arms and fight. Instead, he would guide Arjuna through the war, but Arjuna had to do all the physical fighting. Krishna's subtle message is that God or the fully self-aware Universal consciousness would not participate in the illusion it has created on a physical level directly as itself; instead, it would act through the being (or viewpoint) of Arjuna or any of his other creations. He would provide the right insights to Arjuna at the right time, but it was up to Arjuna to act on them.

He preached the entire Bhagavad Gita to Arjuna but then left the choice of action to Arjuna. Arjuna could have walked off the battlefield of Kurukshetra on that fateful day if he had so decided. For Krishna, while he experienced the Arjuna who stayed and fought the Battle of Kurukshetra, he simultaneously experienced a universe where Arjuna walked away from the battlefield, and a different set of events unfolded.

But then, why did he tell Arjuna in the *Vishwaroopa Darshan* that he had decided everything and Arjuna was only a tool of action? He showed Arjuna that the Pandavas had already won the Battle of Kurukshetra and that Arjuna was only his (Krishna's) instrument of destruction. These actions seem to show a fixed and unchangeable future. Conversely, the fantastic experiences of the Sage Kakbhushundi show that reality is not one fixed flow of events; instead, Krishna or Universal consciousness explores multiple storylines. Kakbhushundi was cursed to become a crow but was blessed with the ability to time travel. He witnessed the Ramayana 11 times and the Mahabharata 16 times, with different variations in the storyline. For example, in the case of the Ramayana, in some storylines, Sita returns to Ayodhya to be crowned queen, and Ram and Sita live happily together (unlike our current version, where

Sita is exiled, and she raises Luv and Kush in the forest). There is one version where Sita is killed in the battle against Ravana, and many more.

Similarly, Sage Kakbhushundi has seen the Mahabharata 16 times with different endings; there are a few where the Kauravas win. We must remember that we see things as the beginning and end of a story, but there are no such fixed points; life goes on even after the ending. The ending is an artificial point we create in our story when we say Rama wins over Ravana as some conclusive event. Life goes on after that, and the story continues without a break. Another way to look at this is that sometimes the good forces win and sometimes the bad ones, and constantly, this cycle of the good to the bad and then back to the good happens. How we narrate a story and choose our starting and ending depends on us.

Another point that Krishna saw intuitively was that while he saw multiple parallel realities through his divine vision occurring simultaneously, his creations saw this as a linear flow of time in terms of *Yugas* and described these as repeating lifetimes and patterns. Hanuman's story of finding Rama's many rings in *Patala Lok* shows that the *Treta Yuga* comes repeatedly. Rama's story occurs repeatedly, with variations like Sage Kakbhushundi saw. There are infinite variations; Sage Kakbhushundi experienced only a few.

But then, as mentioned before, how is it possible that Krishna shows Arjuna the future in the *Vishwaroop*

Darshan? If Arjuna could choose between multiple options, how would Krishna judge which choices Arjuna would make in advance? On his part, Krishna experiences many choices that Arjuna can make and their outcomes in different universes, but how does he know that in this particular localised viewpoint of his own, i.e., as this Arjuna, he will follow a specific path in advance?

Krishna is a master of contradictions and has a purpose for behaving like that. His crucial role is to help us break out of the box of our logical minds. Creating multiple such contradictions is an effective way of doing that. He is the main actor in all his creations, but he has chosen to act according to the localised viewpoint of that creation. So, in the case of Arjuna, he has handed over the reins to the localised character of Arjuna. He guides and coaches Arjuna and even supports him subtly at various points during the battle, but he never directly enters the battlefield. ***In this way, he passes the power of free will to the character of Arjuna he created.***

Krishna cannot be separated from his creations; the creator is embedded within his creations in the world of space and time. We can ask a painter to leave his painting (his creation) and go home, but we cannot ask a dancer to leave his dance behind similarly. ***The dance cannot be separated from the dancer.*** Similarly, Krishna becomes one with all the various Arjunas who experience different storylines. ***As he dances, many storylines emerge. And*** *when he goes silent, everything becomes latent, a bundle of possibilities waiting to come to life.*

There is a more profound point that can help address the dilemma: Is there only one 'Arjuna' in this story? Or are there bundles of possibilities waiting to come to life, and furthermore, many variations of Arjuna come to life? Different decisions are made in each situation, and many Arjunas experience parallel realities. While these Arjunas are similar, they become dissimilar with each branching and as they go through new experiences. There is a localised viewpoint in the story that develops an interesting property called the ego, which holds together the character of that Arjuna during one storyline.

Like this, all the Arjunas in different storylines have an ego holding different stories together. They all refer to themselves as Arjuna but have different experiences and remember their somewhat varying past accordingly. All these Arjunas are a part of Krishna or Universal consciousness. While they cannot interact with each other in the same space and time, but they are all connected at the back as one Universal consciousness. Interestingly, when viewed by someone experiencing these parallel realities at different points in time, like Sage Kakbhushundi, they would call all these parallel avatars Arjuna in different timelines. For Krishna or Universal consciousness, of course, all this is happening simultaneously.

So the question arises: Which Arjuna is the real Arjuna? There is no one real Arjuna. Only Universal consciousness beyond space and time is real; the rest are all illusions. Within these illusions, one individual so created becomes attached or entrenched within one narrative. That person develops an individual ego that holds that story together as one entity going through a series of cause-and-effect events. But if you look closely, you will realise that the Arjuna, along even one storyline, is also changing from moment to moment as new experiences come in. There is actually no 'one Arjuna' in this whole illusory play. ***The existence of the ego itself is part of this illusion and not something real.***

Another way to say this is that you can never step into the same stream twice. Every time you step into the stream, different water molecules (because the earlier water molecules have gone way ahead towards the sea) touch different cells on your skin (as your skin is constantly shedding and replacing cells). But your ego holds together the story of you as the same person stepping into the same stream. It is just a story that you feel comfortable with, and it reduces the complexity of describing the situation. However, this description is fundamentally incorrect as it has many flaws, as pointed out above, but it simplifies communication in our lives.

So, there is no 'one Arjuna,' whether we see it as a person moving in time in one universe or see many parallel realities (non-physical and informational, like in a dream) exploring various options. It is just the way we describe it. There is only one Krishna dancing, but it seems like many Arjunas along different storylines in parallel realities in space and time!

Krishna, or Universal Consciousness, has seen all the past, present, and future and is one with all these variations of Arjuna. Being able to intuitively know (intuition is a different knowing mechanism from what we learn from our senses) all the past, present, and future, he is fully aware of all parallel realities simultaneously. He is one with every falling leaf as he is one with each of our profound emotional experiences in all the parallel universes.

Krishna is also experiencing this moment as a limited being like Arjuna, where he grants the power of choice so Arjuna can make his decisions and experience different outcomes from his limited perspective. These two viewpoints, one as Krishna and the other as Arjuna, are like two sides of the same coin. It is like we are sleeping and dreaming on our bed and participating in the physical and emotional drama in the dream; both are happening simultaneously. Many possibilities happen simultaneously for Universal consciousness, but for its creation, a single storyline is underway where they are making choices, subtly guided by Krishna.

Krishna always shares insights relevant to his creations at a particular time so they can evolve. He did not preach the Bhagavad Gita or give the divine vision of the *Vishwaroopa Darshan* to Duryodhana or even the ever-righteous Yudhishthira. He preached it to Arjuna. Arjuna was ready for this instruction at that point in time. He was aware that the *Vishwaroopa Darshan* would loosen Arjuna's ego, and he would subsequently surrender to Krishna. However, it is important to note that Arjuna always had a choice as to what path he should take.

Krishna knew this universe was a creation of his intentions. An intentional universe has many probabilities, but it has a bias built into it. This is the bias towards goodness, *dharma*, or love that Krishna (or Universal consciousness) builds into the structure. This would mean that the Pandavas would defeat the Kauravas in most realities, but the storyline could have many variations, and Sage Kakbhushundi experienced some of these.

It is all a process of evolution created by Krishna or Universal Consciousness. Krishna has the proper insight and advice for every individual at a specific time in their life. Furthermore, he grants individuals free will to exercise whichever of the possible choices. Being omniscient, he is aware of the probabilities of the various choices the person will make. ***The important thing is that probabilities are in play and not a fixed, deterministic, single-story line.*** This is an infinitely potential playfield where its various creations can explore many options as they experience, learn, and evolve. On the other hand, Krishna explores his infinite dimensions through the multifarious finite creations that are granted the power to play in this playfield.

Like a dancer, Krishna enjoys his skill only when he dances. Krishna experiences the world of space and time only through his creations. An excellent dancer flows with his dance, and every dance is a creative outpouring. No two dance performances are the same. It is his expression of creativity at that moment. Similarly, Krishna flows with his creation, handing over the power of free will to his creation to explore the infinitely potential playfield.

Krishna creates and sets his creations free to explore the infinite bed of potentiality of the current moment. ***While dancing through them, he sets them free!***

Reflections – Three Stages of Evolution of Consciousness

Duryodhana, Yudhishthira, and Krishna demonstrate that human consciousness evolves through three stages. Human consciousness has an evolved egoic experience. We segregate ourselves from our experience and can describe it as such to each other. We can further conceptualise these experiences, label them, and draw theoretical models. Animals, as far as we know, are in a pre-egoic stage. They are not fully able to separate themselves as individuals from the experience. For example, a dog (in all probability) would never be able to say or feel, "I am having this experience." It is primarily merged into the experience. Its life is a series of experiences without any segregated experiencer standing outside, being able to watch this flow, drawing theoretical models, etc. They are more directly involved in the flow of experiences.

The pre-egoic stage evolves into the human ego as part of the evolutionary process. The ego segregates the experiencer from the experience. A human being can say, "I am experiencing this or that." The 'I' in the above statement shows the segregation of the experiencer from what is being experienced. Our ability to distance ourselves from our experience is a big step in evolution.

The 'I' consolidates all our memories and traits we associate with, which we erroneously believe represent our free will. A consolidation of attributes is not something alive to make choices. These consolidated traits, referred to as 'I,' are used by our historical conditioning to repeat themselves. It has no free will in itself, but it makes the individual believe, "I am the doer," which represents the ego state.

We were not born with the ego; we have subtly crafted it and placed it upon ourselves. The sense of "I am the doer," which makes us look and feel very responsible, is often a trap. Until one is not deeply aware of who the 'I' in this statement is, one can end up perpetrating the worst horrors in the world. This is what Duryodhana did; he followed his conditioning to its natural conclusion, and we have its culmination in the Draupadi *cheer haran* incident.

Duryodhana represents the ego-dominated stage where the individual sees everything from a survival or individual gain/loss perspective. As one segregates oneself as an individual 'I', one experiences a tough world where one must fight for survival. No larger cause, purpose, or principle is at play; survival, procreation, reduction in unpleasantness, and maximisation of pleasures in a purposeless mechanical physical reality are the primary goals. Each man for himself is Duryodhana's lifetime training and motto.

At one time before the fateful battle, Arjuna and Duryodhana, cousins of Krishna, reach his palace at around the same time, asking for help on the battleground of Kurukshetra. When they arrived, Krishna was taking an afternoon nap, and the two decided to wait for him to wake up. Since Duryodhana came earlier, he sat near Krishna's head, and Arjuna sat near his feet. After some time, Krishna woke up. He saw Arjuna first sitting at his feet and then saw Duryodhana. Both told him the reason they were there. Krishna agreed to help both of them, as they were his cousins. He gave them a choice; one can have his army, the *Narayani Sena*, and the other can have him on their side. Further, he gave the first choice to Arjuna since he saw him first.

Arjuna asked Krishna to be on his side. Krishna informed Arjuna that though he would be on his side, he would not actively participate in the battle, i.e., he would not physically take up arms or fight. He would, however, guide and counsel him on the battlefield, and he should consider that as he made his choice. Arjuna still chose Krishna, and that is how Krishna became Arjuna's charioteer during the Battle of Kurukshetra. Duryodhana was overjoyed at Arjuna's foolish choice, as it meant he would get the formidable *Narayani Sena*.

For Duryodhana, having only Krishna on his side, especially as he would not actively participate in battle, would be nearly useless; the powerful army mattered to him. He couldn't believe Arjuna's silly choice despite having the first chance. According to him, having a higher material force in one's favour was the key to success. On the other hand, Arjuna knew victory comes to the side of *dharma*, and Krishna is the epitome of *dharma*, so he chose Krishna. This is the core difference between a person who thinks only the material world exists and material force is everything and another who believes that larger forces and principles beyond the material world are much more powerful.

Duryodhana always bet on his physical strength and maximised his physical forces. He thought he was just the body, and by using force, he could dominate others; ethics and principles mattered little to him. For him, the core principle was each man to himself, and the winner takes all. All his activities brought pleasure or power to him and bolstered his ego, which was all that was real for him. He did this without shame and with ruthless abandon.

His upbringing in the palace, surrounded by unlimited pleasures of all varieties, court intrigues, constant inputs from his Uncle Shakuni, etc., taught him that the purpose of his life was to capture the throne of Hastinapur—the prime seat of power—somehow. That would put him in the complete position of power to do as he desired and enjoy life to the fullest. This result was to be achieved by whatever means, going so far as making multiple attempts on his cousin's life.

As he made this decision of Draupadi's *cheer haran*, his value system allowed it, and he felt entitled to execute it. Since childhood, he has been used to throwing tantrums and getting his way through his anger. He easily got upset when his ego felt threatened, and he had aggressive response patterns. Once he had won someone in a game of dice, the person became his slave (the accepted value system of those days) and was supposed to take all directions from him and not argue back; otherwise, the person needed to be taught a lesson. These were his core beliefs. One could say that as long as he was unconscious of his ego-oriented actions, he would repeat the programmes he had been fed with.

Besides this, Duryodhana saw being decisive, aggressive, and grasping as essential traits in a leader, which he tried to emulate. This is why he saw Yudhisthira's approach as servile and unfit for leadership. The individual ego is predominant in this stage, and one tries to control as many variables as possible, sometimes even stepping outside ethical boundaries. Winning is the key, and that strengthens the ego further. While Duryodhana represents the extreme state of being in this "I am the doer" stage, this stage has a spectrum. On one side are people who are ready to go to whatever extent to get what they want, and on the other side are those who live by the rules but are still deeply entrenched in this mindset.

The next stage is Yudhisthira's, who let go of his decisions from an individual ego perspective and allowed a larger principle to operate. I call this *the fly on the cart wheel* stage, where one realises larger forces in the universe and higher principles guide action. As mentioned in the introduction of this book, I had a dream many years ago, which led to my building this view of a fly on the cart wheel. Just to recall the key elements of this view - imagine a fly sitting on the side of a cart wheel of a cart moving from one village to another. As the cart trundles along, the fly sitting on the side of the wheel rim will experience itself moving up and down as the wheel rotates. In such a situation, it could erroneously start to imagine that this up-and-down movement is being created through some actions of its own.

Of course, this can only happen if the fly can segregate itself from its experience, as we humans do. This is just an analogy to make a point, so let's imagine a 'human' fly on this cart wheel that can segregate itself from its experience as we do. It can learn to experience happiness on an upward movement and unhappiness during a downward motion. It can also start holding itself responsible for the up and down movement in some convoluted fashion. But in reality, the cart is moving to a larger purpose; all the fly has to do is let go and enjoy the ride. I will refer to Yudhishthira's stage as a fly on the cart wheel stage, where an individual has realised that larger principles govern the universe and one needs to make oneself subservient to those after dropping one's personalised ego.

Yudhishthira believed in the principles of *dharma*, i.e., doing the right thing and leaving the rest to God. According to him, there was a proper way of doing things, clearly delineated from the wrong ways of doing them. He also stoically accepted what came as his due because of his actions. For example, he went not once but twice to the dice game in Hastinapur, knowing full well that Duryodhana and Shakuni would be up to their tricks. As a *Kshatriya* (warrior class), this was the action expected from him once a neighbouring king invited him for a game of dice. As *Kshatriya dharma* required, "A king or *Kshatriya* is expected to accept any challenge of his counterpart, be it of war, duel, or a devastating game of dice." Most importantly, this invitation came from Dhritarashtra, his uncle and elder, which he could never turn down. He knew the consequences of the game could be very harmful to him and his family, but he adhered to the rules of *dharma* of the day.

In the fly on the fly-on-the-cart wheel stage, one is ready to accept the larger principle and make oneself subservient to it. Yudhishthira did not care whether he gained or lost personally, as he followed the path of *dharma*. He did not experience joy at winning the Battle of Kurukshetra; instead, he experienced deep pain and anguish at the resulting carnage. In his place today, Duryodhana would have been beside himself with joy at his victory. This is because Duryodhana comes to the table from an individual ego-dominated space.

Now, is Yudhishthira entirely in a state of non-doing as he believes larger forces are in action and he is just a fly on the cart wheel? Yudhishthira may still think he has free will, making decisions and choosing one action over another. Yudhishthira does not realise this, but his conditioning drives him, as does Duryodhana's. The critical difference is that Yudhishthira has overcome his personalised whims and fancies, i.e., his personal egoic needs, and has managed to adhere to the more significant principles of *dharma*. He has been able to expand his ego to a larger Universal principle. This is an evolution in terms of human consciousness.

Arjuna also becomes like a fly on the cart wheel when he realises that he is just a tool in Krishna's hand. He surrenders to Krishna and decides to perform his (Arjuna's) duty to the fullest of his abilities without thinking about victory or loss. Giving up the feeling of doership and loosening the ego's grip can be very difficult. One has to trust the universe to do the best for them as they do actions for the larger good, not getting too concerned about personal gain or loss.

The entire process of the evolution of consciousness involves the dissolution of the narrow individualised

ego and increased access to Universal consciousness. When an individual profoundly and truly realises and accepts the infinite power and potential of the eternal current moment or Universal consciousness and understands the smallness of the narrow ego-oriented worlds they are creating and struggling in, the ego automatically dissolves, and deep acceptance arrives. Everything is seen as God's will, and uninterrupted internal calmness and peace are experienced.

Just to be clear, deep acceptance does not mean inaction. This deep acceptance also shows the way forward to the right next step. The individual knows that Universal consciousness understands what is best for them and will show the way forward. When there is a deep trust in this process, the universe never fails to answer that call. ***Some of the highest and most intense action happens when the ego is dissolved.*** Krishna did not ask Arjuna to stop actions; instead, the message was to intensify action but with a different mindset.

Next, as we move to Krishna's state of consciousness, we must contrast his approach with Yudhishthira's. Yudhishthira knows that Krishna has the most profound understanding of *dharma* among all the people known to him, but he could not understand Krishna's actions. Krishna's *dharma* is flexible, whereas Yudhishthira's *dharma* is rigid as it comes from the written words of the scriptures. Krishna's most potent message through the Mahabharata is that *dharma* is conditioned by time, place, and circumstances. As a result, it evolves and is not fixed and rigid. There are no fixed answers and no guidebook to what action one should undertake in every situation. Being in the moment and accepting the current reality, one should act as the situation demands, keeping in mind the highest good of all beings. Duryodhana and his uncle devised multiple ways to get the Pandavas out of the way, and their actions were becoming more unethical and *adharmic*. Somebody had to act to curtail their blatant abuse of *dharma*. Krishna realised the need. Yudhishthira was following the rule book of *dharma*, literally and technically, and was not keen to enter a battle despite the blatant transgressions of his cousins.

Krishna was an evolved soul who had a direct first-hand experience of Universal consciousness. He is the creator and experiencer of all this elusive play of information. He is within all his creation and also outside as eternity beyond space and time. He effortlessly experiences and participates in multiple universes while remaining beyond the limitations of space and time. In this stage, the individual realises he is none other than the creator itself. This is the direct experience of *Aham Bhramasmi* – I am Brahman! Or I am That! Or I am Universal consciousness! Brahman is defined as the Absolute or the Supreme reality.

Krishna simultaneously experiences all possible pasts, presents, and futures in parallel universes. For his true eternal nature, there is no movement of time.

All the possible pasts, presents, and futures are available immediately in the vast eternity of the current moment. These are illusions Krishna creates for his enjoyment. These are not physical universes. These are dreams or virtual worlds arising from the eternal current moment. Through the actions and experiences of Universal consciousness, which splits into multiple individual consciousnesses while choosing to forget their true nature, the world we know (and many more worlds that we will never experience) takes shape and gets experienced.

Universal consciousness creates everything and then accedes to the individual's view in the multiple storylines, becoming one with their viewpoint (like we forget ourselves in a dream and become one with the character in the dream). In the case of humans, ***Universal consciousness grants some freedom of choice through the enhanced level of consciousness, where we constantly make different choices and then explore the consequences of the same.*** This point is significant as it addresses the dilemma of the existence of an individual free will. Notably, less than one per cent of our memory structure is visible to our consciousness; a large part resides in the subconscious and unconscious state, driving our decisions and actions, but remains invisible.

Giving the power of consciousness to an individual and awakening it to some degree, Universal consciousness grants freedom to all individuals to explore different realities as per their choices and decisions. As mentioned before, it does this by conveniently forgetting its true nature and becoming one with the individual's viewpoint. It then explores the infinite diversity of possibilities inherent within it. You could say that Krishna is making decisions, acting from the limited perspective of the individual being after forgetting his Universal nature, or you could say that the individual is acting of their free will; both are the same.

So, all conscious beings have the freedom to explore the highly potential current moment, make decisions, and experience the consequences of their choices. The future is open, and many future paths can be pursued. Krishna empowers the individual to explore different paths and learn and evolve. ***Every being is a mixture of past conditioning (repetitive activity and comfort zones) and exploring freedom at the moment; the battle between these two forces is the process of evolution.*** In this movement, Krishna's approach is not that of a dry observer watching from far away; it is of a highly engaged player who has chosen to forget his true nature after becoming one with his creations.

So, we are not looking at an impersonal God, distantly experiencing multiple destinies; instead, we are dealing with a loving God who first gives up his identity and becomes one with his creation to enjoy the world he has created. Then, he empowers his creation to experiment with different choices while keeping the basic background systems running (like the constant beating of our heart, the flow of our enzymes, etc.) and keeping the being alive. This God explores and learns with us. It is an intentional and loving universe that cares for its creation and wishes to evolve it to its highest potential.

We are all experiencing Krishna *leela*, an illusory play circulating through many lifetimes until we realise who we truly are, i.e., the creator itself, reach *Nirvana*, and merge into the oneness of the creator. There are many ways to speed up this evolution. Here, the process of Yoga is typically proposed. Yoga means "to yoke" or "to unite" the individual consciousness with Universal consciousness. While Yoga readies the body and mind for absorbing its infinite nature, finally, for any realisation to arrive, the creator's grace is essential. At the right time in the process of evolution, the final realisation of Aham Bhrmasmi or 'I am That' finally dawns. This is not a theoretical understanding of an intellectual concept; it is a direct experience of the oneness of the entire existence.

Summarising the three stages of human development: Duryodhana (predominance of the individual ego) ➜ Yudhishthira/Arjuna (surrender to the larger forces in the universe, subsuming one's ego into that—a fly on the cart wheel stage) ➜ Krishna (becoming one with Universal consciousness – Aham Bhramasmi – I am That!).

With this, we come full circle to the question of free will. In the first stage, we experience and believe only in individual free will; everything depends on our decisions as we struggle as lonely individuals fighting it out to survive and procreate. In the second stage, our ego begins to dissolve as we realise all our actions stem from larger forces governing the universe; accepting those and remaining in harmony with them is best for us. In the third stage, we realise we are Universal consciousness itself, creating and experiencing all these informational illusions. Once we realise that we are in an informational illusion or a dream, which is just one of many where our duplicates make different choices, and we are just deciding to be associated with one of the storylines, everything changes in the equation.

As we realise that we are not the storyline but the eternal experiencer beyond space and time, we also realise we are creating our own reality. We move from a position of victimhood to a place of responsibility. *We are responsible for the world we create; this is our choice.* Since we are the eternal experiencer, we are also the same experiencer in every other being and the worlds we are creating therein.

Once we can see the world from everyone's point of view equally, by dissolving our ego, the reasons for others' actions become clear to us. We can genuinely empathise with all, and deep acceptance arises. But this acceptance is not one leading to inaction; instead, it is active acceptance, moving us towards the right action at the moment, the highest action we can perform for the good of all. Being fully enlightened and knowledgeable of everything in the universe, Krishna himself did not stop acting in whatever capacity the world set him up for. He played the role of a mere charioteer for Arjuna in Mahabharata. He built cities and kingdoms and managed all the necessary affairs of the world. Being enlightened does not mean one becomes inactive; instead, one gets even more active and contributes much more. This is the true state of being Aham Bramasmi; I am That!

We are all recyclers of information, learning and evolving as we go through different storylines or multiple lives until we recognise our Universal nature and merge into that. Evolution is an important term here. Evolution is the process of awakening consciousness, our Universal nature. Duryodhana, Yudhisthira, and Krishna represent the three broad stages of evolution within humans.

I close these reflections on the evolution of consciousness with the four *Mahavakyas*, the great sayings, from the ancient Hindu scriptures. The period when these Upanishads are composed where these *Mahavakyas* are quoted is uncertain and contested, but these are ancient texts. There is a wide range from 800 BCE to 200 BCE when these texts would have been composed. This great wisdom was shared by highly evolved souls a very long time ago, and we can choose to ignore it, but it will be our loss only.

Prajnanam Brahman - Consciousness is Brahman (or the Absolute or the Supreme/Ultimate reality) - Aitareya Upanishad 3.3 of the Rig Veda: This first *Mahavakya* says there is none other than consciousness in this Universe, and everything is created and guided by it.

Ayam Atma Brahma - This Self (Atman) is Brahman - (Mandukya Upanishad 1.2 of the Atharva Veda): This *Mahavakya* is quite similar to the first one; only terms of description have changed. The Self, Atman, or Soul are terms for consciousness, and Brahman is the Supreme reality - both are the same. The base of the Universe, the Self, or Universal consciousness, possesses these fundamental qualities—Sat (Truth), Chit (Consciousness), and Ananda (Bliss).

Tat Tvam Asi - Thou Art That - (Chandogya Upanishad of the Sama Veda, as the teacher Uddalaka Aruni instructs his son on the nature of Brahman, the supreme reality): This *Mahavakya* is the same statement stated in the second person. The teacher tells the seeker that his consciousness is the same as the Universal consciousness or absolute reality.

Aham Brahman Asmi - I am Brahman, or I am Divine, or I am That (Brihadaranyaka Upanishad 1.4.10 of the Yajur Veda): Finally, this last *Mahavakya*, as you notice, is the same statement made in the first person. The seeker realises and declares they are Brahman, the absolute reality, or Universal consciousness! There is nothing other that exists!

You will notice that these four short sayings summarise all that is discussed in this book. They address the ultimate nature of our reality quite conclusively. May the greater forces of the universe help you actualise the meaning of these statements in your life!

About the Author

Bhupendra is an engineer, a seasoned business leader, an intense explorer of the nature of reality, and an enthusiastic lover of science. When he is not busy solving the problems of the business world, Bhupendra loves to spend time with people and coach them to maximise their potential. He has had a long-term fascination with the developments at the crossroads of science and spirituality. His secret passion has always been to connect the dots between the outer frontiers of scientific research and the creative and living world of the human spirit.

He promotes the principles of spiritual leadership and calls himself the 'meaning and purpose' guy. At the heart of his philosophy is an alive, intentional, loving, and intelligent universe, which creates and evolves all its creations, including all living and nonliving things. Everyone has a purpose; the question is how to become aware of and manifest it in life. It has been his lifelong dedication to helping people along this path. He has three published books exploring this area.

Bhupendra has had an extensive career of more than two decades with one of the leading multinational corporations. Currently, he is the CEO of a well-known brand in India.

Bhupendra is married and has two sons, currently residing in Hyderabad, India.

www.ingramcontent.com/pod-product-compliance
Lightning Source LLC
Chambersburg PA
CBHW031050160726
47991CB00005B/2099